Informing the legislative debate since 1914

Comprehensive Nuclear-Test-Ban Treaty: Background and Current Developments

Jonathan E. Medalia
Specialist in Nuclear Weapons Policy

September 29, 2014

Congressional Research Service

7-5700

www.crs.gov

RL33548

Summary

A ban on all nuclear tests is the oldest item on the nuclear arms control agenda. Three treaties that entered into force between 1963 and 1990 limit, but do not ban, such tests. In 1996, the United Nations General Assembly adopted the Comprehensive Nuclear-Test-Ban Treaty (CTBT), which would ban all nuclear explosions. In 1997, President Clinton sent the CTBT to the Senate, which rejected it in October 1999. In a speech in Prague in April 2009, President Obama said, "My administration will immediately and aggressively pursue U.S. ratification of the Comprehensive Test Ban Treaty." However, the Administration focused its efforts in 2010 on securing Senate advice and consent to ratification of the New Strategic Arms Reduction Treaty (New START). The Administration has indicated it wants to begin a CTBT "education" campaign with a goal of securing Senate advice and consent to ratification, but there were no hearings on the treaty in the 111th or 112th Congresses, or so far in the 113th. As of September 2014, 183 states had signed the CTBT and 163, including Russia, had ratified it. However, entry into force requires ratification by 44 states specified in the treaty, of which 41 had signed the treaty and 36 had ratified. Eight conferences have been held to facilitate entry into force, most recently on September 27, 2013.

Nuclear testing has a long history, beginning in 1945. The Natural Resources Defense Council states that the United States conducted 1,030 nuclear tests, the Soviet Union 715, the United Kingdom 45, France 210, and China 45. (Of the U.K. tests, 24 were held jointly with the United States and are not included in the foregoing U.S. total.) The last U.S. test was held in 1992; Russia claims it has not tested since 1990. In 1998, India and Pakistan announced several nuclear tests. Each declared a test moratorium; neither has signed the CTBT. North Korea announced that it conducted nuclear tests in 2006, 2009, and 2013. Since 1997, the United States has held 27 "subcritical experiments" at the Nevada National Security Site, most recently in December 2012, to study how plutonium behaves under pressures generated by explosives. It asserts these experiments do not violate the CTBT because they cannot produce a self-sustaining chain reaction. Russia reportedly held some such experiments since 1998.

The Stockpile Stewardship Program seeks to maintain confidence in the safety, security, and reliability of U.S. nuclear weapons without nuclear testing. Its budget is listed as "Weapons Activities" within the request of the National Nuclear Security Administration, a semiautonomous component of the Department of Energy. Congress addresses nuclear weapon issues in the annual National Defense Authorization Act and the Energy and Water Development Appropriations Act. The FY2014 enacted amount for Weapons Activities was $7,781.0 million, and the FY2015 request is $8,314.9 million. Congress also considers a U.S. contribution to a global system to monitor possible nuclear tests, operated by the CTBT Organization Preparatory Commission. The FY2015 request for the contribution was $30.3 million plus a special contribution of $100,000.

This report will be updated occasionally. This update reflects the FY2015 budget request and developments through September 2014. CRS Report RL34394, *Comprehensive Nuclear-Test-Ban Treaty: Issues and Arguments*, by Jonathan E. Medalia, presents pros and cons in detail. CRS Report R40612, *Comprehensive Nuclear-Test-Ban Treaty: Updated "Safeguards" and Net Assessments*, by Jonathan E. Medalia, discusses safeguards—unilateral steps to maintain U.S. nuclear security consistent with nuclear testing treaties—and their relationship to the CTBT. CRS Report R43567, *Energy and Water Development: FY2015 Appropriations*, coordinated by Mark Holt, provides details on stockpile stewardship.

Contents

Tables

Appendixes

Contacts

Most Recent Developments

On September 4, 2014, the Republic of the Congo ratified the Comprehensive Nuclear-Test-Ban Treaty (CTBT). On August 18, the Comprehensive Nuclear-Test-Ban Treaty Organization (CTBTO) Preparatory Commission inaugurated a new facility to train personnel and to test equipment for infrasound (low-frequency sound) and seismic detection of nuclear explosions. A report of August 11 indicated that activity at North Korea's nuclear test site "has come to a standstill," judging from satellite imagery. On June 16-17, the Preparatory Commission held its 42nd meeting; the next is scheduled for October 28-30. The G7 summit held June 4-5 in Brussels adopted a declaration on nonproliferation and disarmament calling, among other things, for early entry into force and universalization of the CTBT. On April 12, Rose Gottemoeller, Undersecretary of State for Arms Control and International Security, spoke in Hiroshima on "The History and Future of the CTBT." On March 4, Niue became the 162nd state to ratify the CTBT.

History

While the CTBT was opened for signature in 1996,[1] it has not entered into force, leaving a ban on nuclear testing as the oldest item on the arms control agenda. Efforts to curtail tests have been made since the 1940s. In the 1950s, the United States and Soviet Union conducted hundreds of hydrogen bomb tests. The radioactive fallout from these tests spurred worldwide protest. These pressures, plus a desire to improve U.S.-Soviet relations in the wake of the Cuban Missile Crisis of 1962, led to the Limited Test Ban Treaty of 1963, which banned nuclear explosions in the atmosphere, in space, and under water. The Threshold Test Ban Treaty, signed in 1974, banned underground nuclear weapons tests having an explosive force of more than 150 kilotons, the equivalent of 150,000 tons of TNT, 10 times the force of the Hiroshima bomb. The Peaceful Nuclear Explosions Treaty, signed in 1976, extended the 150-kiloton limit to nuclear explosions for peaceful purposes. President Carter did not pursue ratification of these treaties, preferring to negotiate a comprehensive test ban treaty, or CTBT, a ban on all nuclear explosions. When agreement on a CTBT seemed near, however, he pulled back, bowing to arguments that continued testing was needed to maintain reliability of existing weapons, to develop new weapons, and for other purposes. President Reagan raised concerns about U.S. ability to monitor the two unratified treaties and late in his term started negotiations on new verification protocols. These two treaties were ratified in 1990.

With the end of the Cold War, the need for improved warheads dropped and pressures for a CTBT grew. The U.S.S.R. and France began nuclear test moratoria in October 1990 and April 1992, respectively. In early 1992, many in Congress favored a one-year test moratorium. The effort led to the Hatfield-Exon-Mitchell amendment to the FY1993 Energy and Water Development Appropriations Bill, which banned testing before July 1, 1993, set conditions on a resumption of testing, banned testing after September 1996 unless another nation tested, and required the President to report to Congress annually on a plan to achieve a CTBT by September 30, 1996.

---

[1] For treaty text and analysis, see U.S. Congress. Senate. *Comprehensive Nuclear Test-Ban Treaty: Message from the President of the United States Transmitting Comprehensive Nuclear Test-Ban Treaty ...*, Treaty Doc. 105-28, September 23, 1997. Washington: GPO, 1997, xvi + 230 p, http://www.gpo.gov/fdsys/pkg/CDOC-105tdoc28/pdf/ CDOC-105tdoc28.pdf, and U.S. Department of State. "Comprehensive Test Ban Treaty (CTBT)," http://www.state.gov/t/isn/trty/16411 htm.

President George H. W. Bush signed the bill into law (P.L. 102-377) October 2, 1992. The CTBT was negotiated in the Conference on Disarmament. It was adopted by the U.N. General Assembly on September 10, 1996, and was opened for signature on September 24, 1996. As of September 2014, 183 states had signed it and 163 had ratified.[2]

National Positions on Testing and the CTBT

United States: Under the Hatfield-Exon-Mitchell amendment, President Clinton had to decide whether to ask Congress to resume testing. On July 3, 1993, he said, "A test ban can strengthen our efforts worldwide to halt the spread of nuclear technology in weapons," and "the nuclear weapons in the United States arsenal are safe and reliable." While testing offered advantages for safety, reliability, and test ban readiness, "the price we would pay in conducting those tests now by undercutting our own nonproliferation goals and ensuring that other nations would resume testing outweighs these benefits." Therefore, he (1) extended the moratorium at least through September 1994; (2) called on other nations to extend their moratoria; (3) said he would direct DOE to "prepare to conduct additional tests while seeking approval to do so from Congress" if another nation tested; (4) promised to "explore other means of maintaining our confidence in the safety, the reliability and the performance of our own weapons"; and (5) pledged to refocus the nuclear weapons laboratories toward technology for nuclear nonproliferation and arms control verification. He extended the moratorium twice more; on January 30, 1995, the Administration announced his decision to extend the moratorium until a CTBT entered into force, assuming it was signed by September 30, 1996.

On September 22, 1997, President Clinton submitted the CTBT to the Senate. He asked the Senate to approve it in his State of the Union addresses of 1998 and 1999. Senate Foreign Relations Committee Chairman Helms rejected that request, saying that the treaty "from a non-proliferation standpoint, is scarcely more than a sham" and had low priority for the committee. In summer 1999, Senate Democrats pressed Senators Helms and Lott to permit consideration of the treaty. On September 30, 1999, Senator Lott offered a unanimous-consent request to discharge the Senate Foreign Relations Committee from considering the treaty and to have debate and a vote. The request, as modified, was agreed to. The Senate Armed Services Committee held hearings October 5-7; the Foreign Relations Committee held a hearing October 7. It quickly became clear that the treaty was far short of the votes for approval, leading many on both sides to seek to delay a vote. As the vote was scheduled by unanimous consent, and several Senators opposed a delay, the vote was held October 13, rejecting the treaty, 48 for, 51 against, and 1 present. At the end of the 106th Congress, pursuant to Senate Rule XXX, paragraph 2, the treaty moved to the Senate Foreign Relations Committee calendar, where it currently resides.

The Bush Administration's Nuclear Posture Review and Nuclear Testing: In the FY2001 National Defense Authorization Act (P.L. 106-398, §1041), Congress directed the Secretary of Defense, in consultation with the Secretary of Energy, to review nuclear policy, strategy, arms control objectives, and the forces, stockpile, and nuclear weapons complex needed to implement U.S. strategy. Although the resulting Nuclear Posture Review is classified, J.D. Crouch, Assistant Secretary of Defense for International Security Policy, presented an unclassified briefing on it on

---

[2] For a current list of signatures and ratifications, see "Status of Signature and Ratification" at the Comprehensive Nuclear Test-Ban-Treaty Organization website, http://www.ctbto.org/the-treaty/status-of-signature-and-ratification/.

January 9, 2002, dealing in part with the CTBT and nuclear testing.[3] He stated there would be "no change in the Administration's policy at this point on nuclear testing. We continue to oppose CTBT ratification. We also continue to adhere to a testing moratorium." Further, "DOE is planning on accelerating its test-readiness program" to reduce the time needed between a decision to test and the conduct of a test, which was then 24 to 36 months. He discussed new weapons. "At this point, there are no recommendations in the report about developing new nuclear weapons ... we are trying to look at a number of initiatives. One would be to modify an existing weapon, to give it greater capability against ... hard targets and deeply-buried targets. And we're also looking at non-nuclear ways that we might be able to deal with those problems." A *Washington Post* article of January 10, 2002, quoted White House Press Secretary Ari Fleischer as saying that the President has not ruled out testing "to make sure the stockpile, particularly as it is reduced, is reliable and safe. So he has not ruled out testing in the future, but there are no plans to do so."[4]

Critics expressed concern about the implications of these policies for testing and new weapons. Physicians for Social Responsibility argued, "The Administration's plan ... would streamline our nuclear arsenal into a war-fighting force, seek the opportunity to design and build new nuclear weapons, and abandon a ten-year-old moratorium on nuclear weapons testing."[5] Another critic felt that increased funding for test readiness would in effect give prior approval for testing.

In July 2002 a National Academy of Sciences panel report on technical aspects of the CTBT concluded, in the words of a press release, "that verification capabilities for the treaty are better than generally supposed, U.S. adversaries could not significantly advance their nuclear weapons capabilities through tests below the threshold of detection, and the United States has the technical capabilities to maintain confidence in the safety and reliability of its existing weapons stockpile without periodic nuclear tests."[6]

A U.N. draft document of August 5, 2005, for signature by heads of government and heads of state at the U.N. General Assembly meeting of September 2005, contained a provision that the signers "resolve to ... [m]aintain a moratorium on nuclear test explosions pending the entry into force of the Comprehensive Nuclear-Test-Ban Treaty and call upon all States to sign and ratify the Treaty."[7] John Bolton, the U.S. Ambassador to the United Nations, reportedly called for major changes to the draft; the CTBT passage was one of many drawing his objection.[8]

On June 25, 2007, Secretary of State Condoleezza Rice stated:

> the Administration does not support the Comprehensive Test Ban Treaty and does not intend to seek Senate advice and consent to its ratification. There has been no change in the

---

[3] U.S. Department of Defense. News Transcript: "Special Briefing on the Nuclear Posture Review," January 9, 2002; see http://www.defenselink.mil/transcripts/2002/t01092002_t0109npr.html.

[4] Walter Pincus, "U.S. Aims for 3,800 Nuclear Warheads," *Washington Post,* January 10, 2002.

[5] Physicians for Social Responsibility, "PSR: Bush Nuclear Weapons Plan Sets Stage for new Bombs, Resumption of Testing; Plan Endangers National Security, Public Health," press release via U.S. Newswire, January 8, 2002.

[6] The National Academies, "Academy Addresses Technical Issues in Nuclear Test Ban Treaty ...," press release, July 31, 2002. The full report, *Technical Issues Related to the Comprehensive Nuclear Test Ban Treaty,* is available at http://www.nap.edu/catalog.php?record_id=10471#toc.

[7] U.N. General Assembly. "Revised draft outcome document of the High-level Plenary Meeting of the General Assembly of September 2005 submitted by the President of the General Assembly," A/59/HLPM/CRP.1/Rev.2, advance unedited version, August 5, 2005.

[8] Julian Borger, "Question Mark over the Summit," *Manila Bulletin,* August 27, 2005.

Administration's policy on this matter. By reducing the likelihood of the need to return to underground nuclear testing, RRW [the Reliable Replacement Warhead] makes it more likely that the United States would be able to continue its voluntary nuclear testing moratorium. We cannot, however, provide guarantees regarding the voluntary moratorium. We may find at some future time that we cannot diagnose or remedy a problem in a warhead critical the U.S. nuclear deterrent without conducting a nuclear test.[9]

Similarly, a Statement of Administration Policy on S. 1547, FY2008 National Defense Authorization Act, included the following:

While supporting the continued voluntary moratorium on testing, the Administration strongly opposes a provision of section 3122 that calls for the ratification of the CTBT. It would be imprudent to tie the hands of a future administration that may have to conduct a test of an element of an aging, unmodernized stockpile in order to assure the reliability of the nuclear deterrent force. Absent such a test, the United States may not be able to diagnose or remedy a problem in a warhead critical to the Nation's deterrent strategy.[10]

The Obama Administration and the CTBT: In a speech in Prague on April 5, 2009, President Obama said, "my administration will immediately and aggressively pursue U.S. ratification of the Comprehensive Test Ban Treaty."[11] Secretary of State Hillary Clinton stated, "The Comprehensive Nuclear-Test-Ban Treaty is an integral part of our non-proliferation and arms control agenda, and we will work in the months ahead both to seek the advice and consent of the United States Senate to ratify the treaty, and to secure ratification by others so that the treaty can enter into force."[12] Secretary of Defense Robert Gates, asked if the United States should ratify the CTBT, replied, "I think that if there are adequate verification measures, probably should."[13]

The Obama Administration released its Nuclear Posture Review (NPR) report in April 2010, which "focuses on five key objectives of our nuclear weapons policies and posture:

1. Preventing nuclear proliferation and nuclear terrorism;

2. Reducing the role of U.S. nuclear weapons in U.S. national security strategy;

3. Maintaining strategic deterrence and stability at reduced nuclear force levels;

4. Strengthening regional deterrence and reassuring U.S. allies and partners; and

5. Sustaining a safe, secure, and effective nuclear arsenal."[14]

---

[9] Letter from Condoleezza Rice, Secretary of State, to Honorable Pete Domenici, United States Senate, June 25, 2007.

[10] U.S. Executive Office of the President. Office of Management and Budget. "Statement of Administration Policy: S. 1547—National Defense Authorization Act for Fiscal Year 2008," p. 7, at http://www.whitehouse.gov/omb/legislative/ sap/110-1/s1547sap-s.pdf.

[11] U.S. White House. Office of the Press Secretary. "Remarks by President Obama," Hradcany Square, Prague, Czech Republic, April 5, 2009, http://www.whitehouse.gov/the_press_office/Remarks-By-President-Barack-Obama-In-Prague-As-Delivered/.

[12] "Secretary of State Hillary Rodham Clinton, Remarks at CTBT Article XIV Conference, New York, NY, September 24, 2009," p. 2, http://www.ctbto.org/fileadmin/user_upload/Art_14_2009/240909_Morning_Session/240909_US.pdf.

[13] Robert Gates, "Nuclear Weapons and Deterrence in the 21st Century," address to the Carnegie Endowment for International Peace, Washington, DC, October 28, 2008.

[14] U.S. Department of Defense. *Nuclear Posture Review Report.* April 2010, p. iii, http://www.defense.gov/npr/docs/ 2010%20Nuclear%20Posture%20Review%20Report.pdf.

Consistent with Administration statements, the report presented the CTBT as a way to implement the first objective. It called several arms control measures, including the CTBT, "a means of strengthening our ability to mobilize broad international support for the measures needed to reinforce the non-proliferation regime and secure nuclear materials worldwide."[15] It viewed ratification and early entry into force of the CTBT as contributing to the prevention of nuclear proliferation and nuclear terrorism:

> Ratification of the CTBT is central to leading other nuclear weapons states toward a world of diminished reliance on nuclear weapons, reduced nuclear competition, and eventual nuclear disarmament. U.S. ratification could also encourage ratification by other states, including China, and provide incentives for the remaining states to work toward entry into force of the treaty. Further, U.S. ratification of the CTBT would enable us to encourage non-NPT Parties to follow the lead of the NPT-recognized Nuclear Weapon States in formalizing a heretofore voluntary testing moratorium, and thus strengthen strategic stability by reducing the salience of nuclear weapons in those states' national defense strategies.[16]

The report also called for a substantial effort to maintain nuclear weapons and to upgrade the workforce and physical infrastructure of the nuclear weapons complex.

Vice President Joseph Biden wrote, "The President has made ratification of the Comprehensive Test Ban Treaty an Administration priority. He has asked me to guide the Administration's effort to gain Senate support for the treaty."[17] Under Secretary of State Ellen Tauscher described elements of the Administration's strategy to win Senate approval of the treaty. "This administration will not attempt to [seek ratification] unless we believe it can actually pass.... [We are] laying the groundwork for the support of a supermajority in the Senate, 67 votes.... We [will] have a very, very short window to talk about CTBT. But when we believe that we have the right conditions, we will begin to engage the Senate."[18]

Obtaining Senate advice and consent to ratification has proven to be a challenge. Senator John Kerry, chairman of the Senate Foreign Relations Committee, stated, "I will begin working to build the necessary bipartisan support for U.S. ratification of the Comprehensive Nuclear Test Ban Treaty ... success would be the single greatest arms control accomplishment for the new Senate and it would reestablish America's traditional leadership role on nonproliferation."[19] On the other hand, Senate Minority Leader Mitch McConnell said, "I also disagree with the administration's recent pledge to ratify the Comprehensive Test Ban Treaty."[20] And Senator Jon Kyl, who led the opposition to the CTBT in 1999, reportedly said, "I will lead the charge against it and I will do everything in my power to see that it is defeated."[21]

---

[15] Ibid., p. vii.

[16] Ibid., p. 13.

[17] Letter from Vice President Joseph R. Biden, Jr., to The Honorable Edward Pastor, Chairman, Subcommittee on Energy and Water Development, Committee on Appropriations, House of Representatives, September 16, 2009.

[18] "Pressing a Broad Agenda for Combating Nuclear Dangers: An Interview with Undersecretary of State for Arms Control and International Security Ellen Tauscher," interviewed by Daniel Horner and Tom Collina, *Arms Control Today,* November 2009, pp. 8-9. Brackets in the quote are from the text of the article.

[19] John Kerry, "New Directions for Foreign Relations," *Boston Globe,* January 13, 2009.

[20] Senator Mitch McConnell, "U.S. Foreign Policy," remarks in the Senate, *Congressional Record,* daily edition, April 27, 2009, p. S4727.

[21] "Push for Controversial Nuke Treaty Expected Next Spring at the Earliest," *The Cable,* October 2, 2009.

The time line for Senate consideration of the CTBT is uncertain. The Administration decided to press for Senate approval of the U.S.-Russian New Strategic Arms Reduction Treaty (New START) before trying to bring up the CTBT. However, New START fell behind schedule. The treaty it would replace, the Strategic Arms Reduction Treaty (START), expired in December 2009. President Obama signed the new treaty in April 2010 and submitted it to the Senate in May. The Senate Committees on Armed Services, Foreign Relations, and Intelligence held hearings on New START, and the Foreign Relations Committee reported it favorably.[22] President Obama reportedly made securing Senate advice and consent to ratification of New START one of his top priorities for the lame duck session of Congress.[23] The Senate passed the resolution of ratification for that treaty on December 22, 2010, 71-26. Subsequently, Administration officials turned more attention to the CTBT. For example, on September 23, 2011, Ellen Tauscher, then Under Secretary of State for Arms Control and International Security, said, "we have begun the process of engaging the Senate. We like to think of our efforts as an 'information exchange' and are working to get these facts [on verification and stockpile stewardship capabilities] out to members and staff, many of whom have never dealt with this Treaty."[24] On September 26, 2012, Rose Gottemoeller, Acting Under Secretary of State for Arms Control and International Security, said, "As we look towards ratification of the CTBT, we acknowledge that the process will not be easy. That said, the New START ratification process reinvigorated interest in the topic of nuclear weapons and arms control on Capitol Hill. I am optimistic that interest will continue as we engage with Members and staff on this Treaty."[25] On September 15, 2014, Gottemoeller, who had been confirmed as Under Secretary of State for Arms Control and International Security, said,

> Now, I will pivot to the question that is asked each and every time this Treaty is discussed: "What is the plan for Senate ratification?"
>
> The answer is simple. First comes education, and then comes discussion and last and most importantly, comes debate. It is only through that process that you get to a place where a vote could happen.
>
> We are reintroducing this Treaty to the American public, since it has been quite some time it has been discussed outside the Capital Beltway. We are and will continue to outline the clear and convincing facts about our ability to maintain the nuclear stockpile without explosive testing and our ability to effectively monitor and verify Treaty compliance. Both Secretary Moniz and General Klotz have spoken about these two issues this afternoon and they are strong allies in this effort.
>
> We are and will continue to make it clear that a global ban on nuclear explosive testing will hinder regional arms races and impede advancements in nuclear stockpiles around the world.
>
> With an emphasis on a healthy, open dialogue, rather than a timeline, we are working with the Senate to re-familiarize Members with the Treaty. A lot of CTBT-related issues have

---

[22] Links to the hearings are available at U.S. Department of State. Bureau of Arms Control, Verification and Compliance. "Senate Hearings for New START," http://www.state.gov/t/avc/rls/c38598 htm. The Senate Foreign Relations Committee's report is available at http://www.gpo.gov/fdsys/pkg/CRPT-111erpt6/pdf/CRPT-111erpt6.pdf.

[23] Mary Beth Sheridan and Walter Pincus, "Sources: $4 Billion Bid to Save START," *Washington Post*, November 13, 2010, p. 3.

[24] U.S. Department of State. Ellen Tauscher, Under Secretary for Arms Control and International Security, remarks at CTBT Article XIV Conference, New York, NY, September 23, 2011, http://www.state.gov/t/us/173890 htm.

[25] Rose Gottemoeller, "The Last U.S. Nuclear Test—20 Years Later: Status and Prospects for the Comprehensive Test Ban Treaty," remarks, Washington, DC, September 26, 2012, http://www.state.gov/t/us/198244 htm.

changed since 1999, but the Senate has changed a lot since then, too. It is up to us, as policymakers and experts before the American people, to practice due diligence in consideration of this Treaty – that means briefings, hearings at the appropriate time, more briefings, trips to Labs, trips to Vienna and the CTBTO, more briefings, etc., etc.. The Senators should have every opportunity to ask questions, many questions, until they are satisfied.

I want to make one thing very clear: this Administration has no intention of rushing this or demanding premature action before we have had a thorough and rigorous discussion and debate.[26]

United Kingdom: The United Kingdom cannot test because it held its nuclear tests for several decades at the Nevada Test Site and does not have its own test site. Its last test was held in 1991. Britain and France became the first of the original five nuclear weapon states to ratify the CTBT, depositing instruments of ratification with the United Nations on April 6, 1998. On February 14, 2002, and February 23, 2006, the United Kingdom conducted subcritical experiments jointly with the United States at the Nevada Test Site.

The United Kingdom and France maintain their own separate stockpile stewardship programs to maintain existing warheads and, if necessary, develop new ones. For example, the U.K. Atomic Weapons Establishment uses two sites: Aldermaston, which conducts R&D and some manufacturing, and Burghfield, which conducts final assembly, maintenance, and decommissioning of warheads.[27] The United Kingdom and France are also pooling stockpile stewardship resources. A declaration from the November 2010 U.K.-French summit announced the decision by the two states

> to collaborate in the technology associated with nuclear stockpile stewardship in support of our respective independent nuclear deterrent capabilities, in full compliance with our international obligations, through unprecedented co-operation at a new joint facility at Valduc in France that will model performance of our nuclear warheads and materials to ensure long-term viability, security and safety – this will be supported by a joint Technology Development Centre at Aldermaston in the UK.[28]

Stockpile stewardship supports the stockpile, but at issue for the United Kingdom is what weapons it will have in the future, and even whether it will have a nuclear force. The U.K. nuclear force consists of Trident II (D-5) missiles aboard four ballistic missile submarines. With the submarines approaching the end of their service lives, at issue is whether to replace them with something other than ballistic missile submarines (e.g., bombers, land-based missiles, or missiles on attack submarines), and if ballistic missile submarines are chosen, whether to build four or fewer.

---

[26] Rose Gottemoeller, Under Secretary of State for Arms Control and International Security, "Verification and Entry Into Force of the CTBT," http://www.state.gov/t/us/2014/231697 htm, remarks prepared for delivery at Embassy of Kazakhstan et al., "Nuclear Weapons Testing: History, Progress, Challenges," conference, Washington, D.C., September 15, 2014.

[27] For further information on the Atomic Weapons Establishment, see its home page, http://www.awe.co.uk/. For information on the French program, see France. Alternative Energies and Atomic Energy Commission. Military Applications Division. "Nuclear Warheads and Nuclear Propulsion," http://www.cea.fr/english_portal/defense/nuclear_warheads_and_nuclear_propulsion2.

[28] UK Prime Minister's Office. "UK-France Summit 2010 Declaration on Defence and Security Co-operation," November 2, 2010, http://www number10.gov.uk/news/statements-and-articles/2010/11/uk%E2%80%93france-summit-2010-declaration-on-defence-and-security-co-operation-56519.

Scotland held a referendum on September 18, 2014, on whether to become an independent country, and chose to remain part of the United Kingdom. Prior to the vote, there was considerable concern over what would become of the U.K. nuclear deterrent if Scotland were to become independent, as all U.K. ballistic missile submarines are based at Faslane, Scotland. In October 2012, Alex Salmond, the leader of the Scottish National Party (SNP), said, "The SNP Government will be bringing forward a white paper on independence which proposes a written constitution for an independent Scotland, and that constitution will have to be ratified by the Scottish Parliament elected in 2016. The SNP position on this is that the constitution should include an explicit ban on nuclear weapons being based on Scottish territory."[29] If Scotland had decided to become independent and to ban nuclear weapons in its territory, it is unclear what steps Britain would have taken regarding its missile submarine force. Indeed, according to one report of October 2012, "The UK defence secretary [Philip Hammond] said he was making no contingency plans for moving Trident out of Scotland in the event of its people voting yes to independence."[30] Another view put forward in August 2014 was that the Trident base could be relocated to a site within England.[31] However, Scotland's vote to remain part of the United Kingdom has rendered these concerns moot.

France: On June 13, 1995, President Jacques Chirac announced that France would conduct eight nuclear tests at its test site at Mururoa Atoll in the South Pacific, finishing by the end of May 1996. The armed services had reportedly wanted the tests to check existing warheads, validate a new warhead, and develop a computer system to simulate warheads to render further testing unneeded. Many nations criticized the decision. On August 10, 1995, France indicated it would halt all nuclear tests once the test series was finished and favored a CTBT that would ban "any nuclear weapon test or any other nuclear explosion."[32] France conducted six tests from September 5, 1995, to January 27, 1996. On January 29, 1996, Chirac announced the end to French testing. On April 6, 1998, France and Britain deposited instruments of ratification of the CTBT with the United Nations. See the section on the United Kingdom, above, for information on a U.K.-French collaboration on stockpile stewardship.

Russia: Several press reports between 1996 and 1999 claimed that Russia may have conducted low-yield nuclear tests at its Arctic test site at Novaya Zemlya; other reports stated that U.S. reviews of the data determined that these events were earthquakes. Several reports between 1998 and 2000 stated that Russia had conducted "subcritical" nuclear experiments, discussed below, which the CTBT does not bar. The report of the Congressional Commission on the Strategic Posture of the United States presents arguments for and against the CTBT; one argument by opponents is, "Apparently Russia and possibly China are conducting low yield tests."[33] This

---

[29] Scottish National Party, "Explicit Ban on Nuclear Weapons in Scotland," October 7, 2012, http://www.snp.org/media-centre/news/2012/oct/explicit-ban-nuclear-weapons-scotland.

[30] "No Plan to Move Trident from Clyde, Says UK Minister Hammond," BBC News, October 29, 2012, http://www.bbc.co.uk/news/uk-scotland-scotland-politics-20121173.

[31] Richard Norton-Taylor, "Trident missiles 'could be relocated to Plymouth from independent Scotland,'" *The Guardian,* August 13, 2014, http://www.theguardian.com/uk-news/2014/aug/14/trident-missiles-relocate-plymouth-independent-scotland-rusi-report.

[32] Craig Whitney, "France to Back Ban After Its Atom Tests," *New York Times,* August 11, 1995, p. 3.

[33] Congressional Commission on the Strategic Posture of the United States, *America's Strategic Posture,* Washington, DC, United States Institute of Peace Press, 2009, p. 83.

charge was reiterated in a September 2011 article: "Russia apparently has continued to test nuclear weapons at very low yields, despite its commitment not to do so."[34]

Russia ratified the treaty on June 30, 2000. In September 2005, Russia reportedly stated that it intends to continue to observe the moratorium on testing until the CTBT enters into force as long as other nuclear powers do likewise, and expressed its hope that the nations that must ratify the treaty for it to enter into force will do so as soon as possible.[35] In November 2007, according to Itar-Tass, Russian Foreign Minister Sergei Lavrov "confirmed Russia's unchanging support for the treaty as one of the key elements of the nuclear non-proliferation regime and an effective nuclear arms limitation tool."[36] In September 2009, Dmitry Medvedev, president of the Russian Federation, said, "we need to encourage leading countries to sign and ratify the Comprehensive Nuclear-Test-Ban Treaty as soon as possible in order to ensure its ultimate entry into force. That is very important."[37]

A Russian scholar at the Russian Academy of Sciences raised the prospect of the CTBT's collapse in an article of November 2010. Claiming that Britain and France have ratified the treaty but do not have a moratorium on testing, that the reverse is the case for China and the United States, that India, Israel, North Korea, and Pakistan have done neither, and that only Russia has ratified the treaty and has a moratorium on testing, he argued that

> if the treaty has not been in force for fifteen years [i.e., since it was opened for signature in 1996], it is difficult for Russia to be the only nuclear power which complies with its terms and conditions in full. Russia's official position is to support the CTBT's entry into force. However, Russian experts tend to focus on the pessimistic scenarios of CTBT collapse. In the near future, Russia could face a difficult choice between the political dividends the CTBT affords and the military necessity to upgrade its nuclear capabilities.[38]

At the 2011 Conference on Facilitating the Entry into Force of the Comprehensive Nuclear-Test-Ban Treaty, Sergey Ryabkov, Deputy Minister of Foreign Affairs of the Russian Federation, expressed his country's support for the treaty and said, "We hope that our call upon the respective States to sign and/or ratify the CTBT will finally be heard by them."[39]

---

[34] R. James Woolsey and Keith Payne, "Reconsidering the Comprehensive Test Ban Treaty," *National Review Online,* September 8, 2011, http://www.nationalreview.com/articles/276530/reconsidering-comprehensive-test-ban-treaty-r-james-woolsey.

[35] "Russia Intends to Continue Moratorium on Nuclear Tests," *BBC Monitoring Former Soviet Union,* excerpt from a report by Russian News Agency ITAR-TASS, September 23, 2005.

[36] "Russia Supports CTBT as Key Element of Nuclear Non-Proliferation—FM," *Itar-Tass,* November 12, 2007.

[37] United Nations. Security Council. 6191st meeting, September 24, 2009, S/PV.6191, provisional version, p. 7.

[38] Alexei Fenenko, Leading Research Fellow, Institute of International Studies, Russian Academy of Sciences, "Russia and the Future of the CTBT," *RIA Novosty,* November 3, 2010, http://en.rian ru/valdai_op/20101103/161192733 htm. Note that France dismantled its nuclear test site: "Two-thirds of French Mururoa N-test Site Dismantled," *Reuters,* September 13, 1997. The 1997 article quotes the site commander as saying that dismantlement would be completed by July 1998. Also, the United Kingdom conducted all its nuclear tests at the Nevada Test Site for many years, so it could not conduct tests unless it were to build its own test site or the United States were to end its nuclear test moratorium.

[39] Russian Federation. Permanent Mission to the United Nations. "Statement by the Head of Delegation of the Russian Federation, Deputy Foreign Minister Sergey A. Ryabkov, at the 7th Conference on Facilitating the Entry into Force of the Comprehensive Nuclear-Test-Ban Treaty," New York, September 23, 2011, http://www.ctbto.org/fileadmin/user_upload/Art_14_2011/Statements/Russia.pdf.

China: China did not participate in the moratorium. It conducted a nuclear test on October 5, 1993, that many nations condemned. It countered that it had conducted 39 tests, as opposed to the 1,054 that the United States had conducted, and needed a few more for safety and reliability. According to one report, "China will immediately stop nuclear testing once the treaty on the complete ban of nuclear tests takes effect, [Chinese Premier] Li Peng said."[40] It conducted other tests on June 10 and October 7, 1994, May 15 and August 17, 1995, and June 8 and July 29, 1996. It announced that the July 1996 test would be its last, as it would begin a moratorium on July 30, 1996. On February 29, 2000, the Chinese government submitted the CTBT to the National People's Congress for ratification. In a white paper of December 2004, China stated its support of early entry into force and, until that happens, its commitment to the test moratorium. As of September 2014, China had not ratified the treaty.

India: On May 11, 1998, Prime Minister Atal Behari Vajpayee announced that India had conducted three nuclear tests. The government stated, "The tests conducted today were with a fission device, a low yield device and a thermonuclear device.... These tests have established that India has a proven capability for a weaponised nuclear programme."[41] It announced two more tests May 13. An academic study concluded, based on seismic data, that India and Pakistan overstated the number and yields of their tests. India has conducted no tests since May 1998, but questioned whether the United States should expect India to sign a treaty that the United States views as flawed. In an Indian-Pakistani statement of June 20, 2004, "Each side reaffirmed its unilateral moratorium on conducting further nuclear test explosions" barring "extraordinary events."[42] On December 22, 2005, Shri Rao Inderjit Singh, Minister of State in the Ministry of External Affairs, said, "India has already stated that it will not stand in the way of the Entry into Force of the Treaty."[43] On August 16, 2007, India's External Affairs Minister, Pranab Mukherjee, reportedly told Parliament, "India has the sovereign right to test and would do so if it is necessary in national interest."[44]

A statement on U.S.-Indian nuclear cooperation of July 18, 2005, by President Bush and Indian Prime Minister Manmohan Singh, said, "The Prime Minister conveyed that for his part, India would reciprocally agree that it would be ready to ... continu[e] India's unilateral moratorium on nuclear testing."[45] In a Senate hearing of November 2, Robert Joseph, Under Secretary of State for Arms Control and International Security, stated, "India's pledge to maintain its nuclear testing moratorium contributes to nonproliferation efforts by making its ending of nuclear explosive tests one of the conditions of full civil nuclear cooperation."[46] At that hearing, Michael Krepon, co-

---

[40] "Li Peng: China's Nuclear Tests Pose No Threat," *Xinhua,* October 8, 1995, in FBIS-TAC-95-006, December 6, 1995, p. 13.

[41] India. Ministry of External Affairs. Press statement, New Delhi, May 11, 1998, at http://nuclearweaponarchive.org/India/Indianofficial.txt.

[42] India. Ministry of External Affairs. "Joint Statement, India-Pakistan Expert-Level Talks on Nuclear CBMs [Confidence-Building Measures]," June 20, 2004.

[43] India. Ministry of External Affairs. Rajya Sabha. Unstarred Question No. 3260, to be answered on December 12, 2005, by Rao Inderjit Singh, Minister of State in the Ministry of External Affairs. http://164.100.24.219/rsq/quest.asp?qref=108782.

[44] "Pranab Mukherjee Says India Has Sovereign Right to Conduct Nuclear Test," *AndhraNews.net,* August 16, 2007; available at http://www.andhranews net/India/2007/August/16-Pranab-Mukherjee-says-11996.asp.

[45] U.S. White House. "Joint Statement Between President George W. Bush and Prime Minister Manmohan Singh," July 18, 2005, at http://www.whitehouse.gov/news/releases/2005/07/20050718-6 html.

[46] U.S. Congress. Senate. Committee on Foreign Relations. Hearing, *Implications of U.S.-India Nuclear Energy Cooperation,* statement by Robert Joseph, Under Secretary of State for Arms Control and International Security, (continued...)

---

founder of the Stimson Center, argued that statements by Indian government officials that there are no current plans to test "do not carry equal weight, nor do they impose equal responsibility, to the obligations accepted by the 176 states that have signed the CTBT."[47] Press reports of April 2006 said the sides were negotiating a detailed nuclear cooperation agreement. The reports indicated that the United States would insist that India maintain its nuclear test moratorium or else the United States would have the right to terminate the agreement. India responded that it had pledged to maintain the moratorium, rendering this provision out of place in the final agreement. A press report of January 2007 quoted National Security Advisor M.K. Narayanan as saying, "There is no question of signing the Comprehensive Test Ban Treaty. We have our voluntary moratorium. That position remains."[48] According to a report of November 2007, when some members of Parliament criticized the U.S.-Indian nuclear agreement on grounds it would bar Indian nuclear testing, Prime Minister Manmohan Singh responded, "If a necessity for carrying out a nuclear test arises in future, there is nothing in the agreement which prevents us from carrying out tests."[49] (See CRS Report R42948, *U.S.-India Security Relations: Strategic Issues*, by K. Alan Kronstadt and Sonia Pinto.)

In August 2009, a former Indian official said that India should not be "railroaded" into signing the CTBT because its hydrogen bomb tests of 1998 did not produce the desired yield. Accordingly, he said, India "should conduct more nuclear tests which are necessary from the point of view of security."[50] In response, other Indian officials claimed that the thermonuclear tests were successful, so no further tests were needed.[51] In December 2009, in response to "the renewed pressure from President Obama on [India] in recent months to sign the CTBT," 11 scientists and others formerly in the Indian nuclear weapons program urged the Indian government not to sign the treaty.[52] In October 2010, a trade agreement in which Japan would sell civilian nuclear technology to India had stalled as Japan urged India to take steps toward signing the CTBT.[53] Meanwhile, India continues to develop its nuclear weapons program. For example, press reports in 2014 described construction in India of a nuclear-powered submarine designed to carry nuclear-armed ballistic missiles,[54] a test of this type of missile,[55] construction of an Indian

---

(...continued)

November 2, 2005. Transcript by CQ Transcriptions, Inc.

[47] U.S. Congress. Senate. Committee on Foreign Relations. Hearing, *Implications of U.S.-India Nuclear Energy Cooperation*, statement by Michael Krepon, Co-Founder, The Henry L. Stimson Center, November 2, 2005. Transcript by CQ Transcriptions, Inc.

[48] "India Not to Accept Any Legal Binding on N-Testing," *Press Trust of India Limited*, January 13, 2007.

[49] "Indian Lawmakers Attack U.S. Nuclear Deal," *Global Security Newswire*, November 29, 2007,

[50] "No CTBT, India Needs More Nuclear Tests: Pokhran II Coordinator," *The Times of India*, August 27, 2009.

[51] "Top Indian Scientists Say Nuclear Tests Were Successful," *Global Security Newswire*, September 25, 2009.

[52] P.K. Iyengar et al., "On Thermonuclear Weapon Capability and Its Implications for Credible Minimum Deterrence: Statement by Deeply Concerned Senior Scientists," *Mainstream*, December 26, 2009, http://www.mainstreamweekly.net/article1865.html.

[53] "Japan-India Atomic Trade Talks Stall over CTBT," *Global Security Newswire*, October 26, 2010, http://gsn.nti.org/gsn/nw_20101026_7486.php.

[54] Pallava Bagla, Vishnu Som, "NDTV Exclusive: This is INS Arihant, First Made-in-India Nuclear Submarine," August 20, 2014, *NDTV.com*, http://www.ndtv.com/article/india/ndtv-exclusive-this-is-ins-arihant-first-made-in-india-nuclear-submarine-578949?curl=1408544078.

[55] "India Reveals Secret Underwater Test-Launch of Ballistic Missile," *Global Security Newswire*, May 12, 2014, http://www.nti.org/gsn/article/india-reveals-secret-underwater-test-launch-ballistic-missile/.

---

uranium enrichment plant,[56] and a test of a missile defense interceptor.[57] As of September 2014, India had not signed the CTBT.

Pakistan: Pakistan announced on May 28, 1998, that it had conducted five nuclear tests, and announced a sixth on May 30. Reports placed the yields of the smallest devices between zero and a few kilotons, and between 2 and 45 kilotons for the largest. Some question the number of tests based on uncertain seismic evidence. Pakistan made no claims of testing fusion devices. Pakistan's weapons program apparently relies heavily on foreign technology. Pakistan claimed that it tested "ready-to-fire warheads," not experimental devices, and included a warhead for the Ghauri, a missile with a range of 900 miles, and low-yield tactical weapons. In response to the Indian and Pakistani tests, the United States imposed economic sanctions on the two nations. In November 1999, Foreign Minister Abdul Sattar said that his nation would not sign the CTBT unless sanctions were lifted, but that "[w]e will not be the first to conduct further nuclear tests."[58] In August 2000, President Pervez Musharraf said the time was not ripe to sign the CTBT because so doing could destabilize Pakistan.[59] In September 2005, Pakistan reportedly said it would not be the first nation in the region to resume nuclear testing.[60] In April 2007, Pakistan's Prime Minister, Shaukat Aziz, reportedly said that Pakistan would not unilaterally sign the CTBT since it shares a border with India.[61] Replying to the statement on nuclear testing by Pranab Mukherjee, India's External Affairs Minister, Tasnim Aslam, a spokeswoman for Pakistan's Foreign Office, reportedly said, "We take seriously the assertions by the Indian leadership about the possibility of renewing nuclear tests.... Resumption of nuclear tests by India would create a serious situation obliging Pakistan to review its position and to take action, appropriate, consistent to our supreme national interest."[62] According to a press report of June 2009, the situation had changed: "'Let me tell you, Pakistan has no plan to sign the CTBT,' Pakistani Foreign Ministry spokesman Abdul Basit said, adding that circumstances have changed since Islamabad pledged in 1998 to sign off on the agreement if nuclear rival India did the same."[63] Meanwhile, like India, Pakistan continues development of its nuclear weapons program. Reports of 2014 describe the start of operations of a third plutonium reactor, with a fourth apparently still under construction[64] and the test firing of a ballistic missile.[65] As of September 2014, Pakistan had not signed the CTBT.

---

[56] David Albright and Serena Kelleher-Vergantini, "India's New Uranium Enrichment Plant in Karnataka," Institute for Science and International Security, July 1, 2014, http://www.isis-online.org/uploads/isis-reports/documents/ SMEF_Brief_July_1_2014_FINAL.pdf.

[57] "Success Questioned in Much-Hyped Indian Antimissile Test," *Global Security Newswire,* May 15, 2014, http://www.nti.org/gsn/article/indias-much-hyped-intercept-test-might-not-have-been-such-success/.

[58] Kathy Gannon, "New Pakistani Government Gives First Official Foreign Policy Statement," newswire, Associated Press, November 8, 1999.

[59] Shahid-ur-Rehman Khan, "Signing CTBT Can Destabilize Pakistan, Says Musharraf," newswire, Kyodo News International, Inc., August 17, 2000.

[60] "Pakistan Today Said It Will Abide by Its 'Solemn Pledge' That It Would Not Be the First Country in the Region to Resume Nuclear Tests ...," newswire, *Press Trust of India Limited,* September 26, 2005.

[61] "Pak Says No to Signing NPT, CTBT Unilaterally," Press Trust of India Limited, April 26, 2007.

[62] "Pakistan Would Consider Nuclear Test If India Tests," *Reuters,* August 20, 2007, available at http://in.reuters.com/ article/topNews/idINIndia-29063920070820.

[63] "Pakistan Rules Out Test Ban Treaty Endorsement," *Global Security Newswire,* June 19, 2009.

[64] Zia Mian, "Pakistan Begins Operating Third Khushab Plutonium Production Reactor," International Panel on Fissile Materials IFPM Blog, June 30,2014, http://fissilematerials.org/blog/2014/06/pakistan_begins_operating html.

[65] "Pakistan Test Fires Nuclear-Capable Ballistic Missile," Post TV/Reuters, April 22, 2014, http://www.washingtonpost.com/posttv/national/pakistan-test-fires-nuclear-capable-ballistic-missile/2014/04/22/ 32f003d2-ca02-11e3-b81a-6fff56bc591e_video.html.

The North Korean Nuclear Tests

The October 2006 Nuclear Test

Negotiations to halt North Korea's nuclear program have been underway for years, most recently between that nation, the United States, China, Japan, South Korea, and Russia (Six-Party Talks). A CIA report of late 2004 stated that during talks in April 2003, "North Korea privately threatened to 'transfer' or 'demonstrate' its nuclear weapons."[66] On February 10, 2005, North Korea declared, "We ... have manufactured nukes for self-defence to cope with the Bush administration's evermore undisguised policy to isolate and stifle North Korea,"[67] and on June 9 it claimed it was building more such weapons. On May 15, 2005, the United States warned that it and other nations would take punitive action if North Korea conducted a nuclear test.[68] In a joint statement from the Six-Party Talks in September 2005, North Korea "committed to abandoning all nuclear weapons and existing nuclear programs and returning, at an early date, to the Treaty on the Non-Proliferation of Nuclear Weapons and to IAEA safeguards."[69] In November 2005, North Korea began a boycott of the talks. On October 3, 2006, North Korea stated that it "will, in the future, be conducting a nuclear test."[70] In response, Japan, the United Kingdom, and the United States warned of consequences if North Korea conducted a test; South Korea expressed "deep regret and concern." For updates on the Six-Party Talks, see CRS Report R41259, *North Korea: U.S. Relations, Nuclear Diplomacy, and Internal Situation*, by Emma Chanlett-Avery and Ian E. Rinehart.

On October 9, 2006, North Korea declared that it had conducted an underground nuclear test. One report placed the yield at as little as 0.2 kilotons.[71] According to other reports, South Korean geologists placed the explosive yield at 550 tons of TNT equivalent (0.55 kilotons),[72] the French Atomic Energy Commission's estimate was 0.50 kilotons,[73] and Russian Minister of Defense Sergei Ivanov placed the yield at 5 to 15 kilotons.[74] For comparison, the Hiroshima bomb had a yield of 15 kilotons. A yield of less than a kiloton is well below the 9 or more kilotons of other nations' first nuclear tests,[75] and below the 4 kilotons that North Korea reportedly told China that

---

[66] "Attachment A: Unclassified Report to Congress on the Acquisition of Technology Relating to Weapons of Mass Destruction and Advanced Conventional Munitions, 1 July Through 31 December 2003." Note: "The Director of Central Intelligence (DCI) hereby submits this report in response to a congressionally directed action in Section 721 of the FY1997 Intelligence Authorization Act ...," c. 2004, p. 5.

[67] "Korean Central News Agency North Korea February 10," *The Guardian*, February 12, 2005.

[68] David Sanger, "U.S. in Warning to North Korea on Nuclear Test," *New York Times*, May 16, 2005, p. 1.

[69] "Joint Statement of the Fourth Round of the Six-Party Talks," Beijing, September 19, 2005, at http://www.state.gov/r/pa/prs/ps/2005/53490 htm.

[70] Democratic People's Republic of Korea, Foreign Ministry Statement, Pyongyang Korean Central Broadcasting Station, October 3, 2006.

[71] "White House Casts Doubt on N. Korean Nuclear Arms," *Reuters* newswire, October 10, 2006.

[72] Evan Ramstad, Jay Solomon, and Gordon Fairclough, "Bomb Fallout: Explosion by North Koreans Imperils Nuclear-Control Effort," *Wall Street Journal*, October 10, 2006, p. 1.

[73] Michael Abramowitz and Colum Lynch, "U.S. Urges Sanctions on North Korea," *Washington Post*, October 10, 2006, in graphic, "North Korea's Big Test," p. 13.

[74] William Broad and Mark Mazzetti, "Blast May Be Only a Partial Success, Experts Say," *New York Times*, October 10, 2006, p. 8.

[75] James Sterngold, "U.S. Urges Sanctions to Restrain North Korea," *San Francisco Chronicle*, October 10, 2006, p. 1.

---

it expected.[76] On October 16, the Office of the Director of National Intelligence released a statement on the test: "Analysis of air samples collected on October 11, 2006 detected radioactive debris which confirms that North Korea conducted an underground nuclear explosion in the vicinity of P'unggye on October 9, 2006. The explosion yield was less than a kiloton."[77]

Most U.S. observers cited in news reports believe that the event was a small nuclear explosion, but at most a partial success. One hypothesis is that, through poor design, the device did not implode properly, greatly reducing its yield.[78] Other hypotheses are that the device reduced the amount of plutonium used in order to conserve that material, or engineers sought to test the design rather than yield of the device, or the device was smaller and more sophisticated than anticipated.[79] On the latter point, Siegfried Hecker, former director, Los Alamos National Laboratory, stated that the North Korean weapon designers most likely did not test a Nagasaki-type device (a basic implosion device) because they could have had high confidence, without testing, that such a device would work. Instead, his analysis is that the North Koreans most likely tested a more advanced design, even at the risk of partial failure, which is what the seismic signals appear to confirm. He considers it highly unlikely that they intentionally designed a mini-nuke. However, even if the test was not fully successful, he believes they learned much from the test.[80]

A more advanced warhead would be of greater military value to North Korea than a Nagasaki bomb because a missile could carry it, but further tests might well be needed to make the warhead militarily usable. The press carried reports that North Korea said it would not conduct further tests, but according to another report, Secretary of State Condoleezza Rice said that Chinese officials, briefing her on the North Korean situation, said nothing about a North Korean test halt.[81] It would take some time to prepare for another test by determining the lessons of the first test, redesigning the device, and testing components of the new design. A moratorium during that time would have little if any impact on its test program.

The seismic record of the North Korean test, when compared with recordings of a 2002 earthquake recorded at a seismic station in Wonju, Republic of Korea, shows differences in seismic wave patterns that are diagnostic of an explosive source.[82] For example, seismic waves from the earthquake build up over several seconds, while waves from the explosion arrive suddenly. Once the amplitudes are measured, the yield may be estimated, but this is complicated by factors such as the local geology and the specifics of the burial. Arthur Lerner-Lam, Associate Director for Seismology, Geology, and Tectonophysics, Lamont-Doherty Earth Observatory, Columbia University, said that the seismic record is not useful for determining whether the event

---

[76] Broad and Mazzetti, "Blast May Be Only a Partial Success, Experts Say."

[77] U.S. Office of the Director of National Intelligence. Public Affairs Office. "Statement by the Office of the Director of National Intelligence on the North Korea Nuclear Test," October 16, 2006, ODNI News Release No. 19-06, 1 p.

[78] Dafna Linzer and Thomas Ricks, "U.S. Waits for Firm Information on Nature and Success of Device," *Washington Post,* October 11, 2006, p. 14.

[79] Dafna Linzer, "Low Yield of Blast Surprises Analysts," *Washington Post,* October 10, 2006, p. 12.

[80] Personal communication, October 13, 2006.

[81] Burt Herman, "U.S. Says No Sign of NKorea Promise Not to Test; SKorea's Ex-President Warns of Backlash," *Associated Press Newswires,* October 21, 2006.

[82] For the two seismographs, see "The CTBT Verification Regime Put to the Test—The Event in the DPRK on 9 October 2006," Comprehensive Nuclear-Test-Ban Treaty Preparatory Commission, at http://www.ctbto.org/ press_centre/featured_articles/2007/2007_0409_dprk htm. For a detailed discussion of the seismic record of the North Korean test, see Paul Richards and Won-Young Kim, "Seismic Signature," *Nature Physics,* January 2007, pp. 4-6.

was a nuclear or conventional explosion without making additional assumptions or inferences.[83] Mining explosions are typically detonated over several seconds in order to break rock efficiently, so their seismological signature can be interpreted in terms of such "ripple firing." However, if North Korea attempted to mimic the signature of a nuclear explosion by setting off all the explosive at the same time, Lerner-Lam said, it would be virtually impossible to discriminate between conventional and nuclear explosions using seismological data alone. Complementary observations provide more direct evidence. A nuclear explosion releases radioactive isotopes of certain gases. They may take days to reach the surface, but once they dissipate into the atmosphere, he said, they may be detected by specially equipped aircraft or ground stations.[84]

The ability of the seismic network to detect an explosion that most sources place at or below one kiloton, and in one case as low as one-fifth of a kiloton, may hold implications for the CTBT. The treaty's supporters claim that the ability to detect subkiloton tests should negate arguments against the treaty on grounds of inadequate monitoring capability. The Comprehensive Nuclear-Test-Ban Treaty Organization Preparatory Commission, for example, states, "the CTBT verification regime proved that it was capable of meeting the expectations set for it,"[85] even though the test was low yield, the IMS was 60% completed, and the noble gas system was 25% completed.[86] Critics respond that the test was not evasively conducted; that evasion scenarios, such as testing during an earthquake or in a large underground cavity, could defeat monitoring efforts; and that subkiloton tests could aid in developing nuclear weapons.

The May 2009 Nuclear Test

North Korea announced on May 25, 2009, that it had conducted a second nuclear test.[87] The U.S. Office of the Director of National Intelligence stated: "The U.S. Intelligence Community assesses that North Korea probably conducted an underground nuclear explosion in the vicinity of P'unggye on May 25, 2009. The explosion yield was approximately a few kilotons. Analysis of the event continues."[88] The lack of certainty on whether the test was nuclear arises because seismic signals, including those detected by 61 stations of the International Monitoring System (IMS, described below),[89] were consistent with a nuclear test, and seismic signals from the 2006 and 2009 events were very similar,[90] but open sources did not report the detection of physical

---

[83] Personal communication, October 10, 2006.

[84] For a technical analysis of the North Korean test, see Richard Garwin and Frank von Hippel, "A Technical Analysis: Deconstructing North Korea's October 9 Nuclear Test," *Arms Control Today,* November 2006.

[85] "The CTBT Verification Regime Put to the Test—The Event in the DPRK on 9 October 2006." This source also has links to many documents on the North Korean test.

[86] Information provided by CTBTO PrepCom, personal communication, February 15, 2008.

[87] For further information on North Korea' nuclear program, see CRS Report RL33590, *North Korea's Nuclear Weapons Development and Diplomacy,* by Larry A. Niksch, and CRS Report RL34256, *North Korea's Nuclear Weapons: Technical Issues,* by Mary Beth D. Nikitin.

[88] U.S. Office of the Director of National Intelligence. Public Affairs Office. "Statement by the Office of the Director of National Intelligence on North Korea's Declared Nuclear Test on May 25, 2009," ODNI News Release No. 23-09, June 15, 2009, at http://www.dni.gov/press_releases/20090615_release.pdf .

[89] Comprehensive Nuclear-Test-Ban Treaty Preparatory Commission, "Homing in on the Event," May 29, 2009, http://www.ctbto.org/press-centre/highlights/2009/homing-in-on-the-event/.

[90] For seismograms of these two events and an earthquake from the same region, see Won-Young Kim, Paul Richards, and Lynn Sykes, "Discrimination of Earthquakes and Explosions Near Nuclear Test Sites Using Regional High-Frequency Data," poster SEISMO-27J presented at the International Scientific Studies conference, June 2009, http://www.ctbto.org/fileadmin/user_upload/ISS_2009/Poster/SEISMO-27J%20%28US%29%20-
(continued...)

---

evidence that would provide conclusive proof of a nuclear test, such as radioactive isotopes of noble gases, especially those having short half-lives, or radioactive particulates (i.e., fallout). For example, the CTBTO Preparatory Commission stated:

> The detection of radioactive noble gas, in particular xenon, could serve to corroborate the seismic findings. Contrary to the 2006 announced DPRK nuclear test, none of the CTBTO's noble gas [detection] stations have detected xenon isotopes in a characteristic way that could be attributed to the [2009] DPRK event so far, even though the system is working well and the network's density in the region is considerably higher than in 2006....
>
> Nor have CTBTO Member States using their own national technical means reported any such measurements. Given the relatively short half-life of radioactive xenon (between 8 hours and 11 days, depending on the isotope), it is unlikely that the [International Monitoring System] will detect or identify xenon from this event after several weeks.[91]

Possible reasons why no radioactive effluents were detected include progress in containment of such effluents by North Korea, drawing on lessons learned from the 2006 test; detailed study of the geology at the test site to locate the test away from potential pathways by which the effluents could reach the surface; release of effluents below the threshold of detection; the possibility that the test was a large chemical explosion; good luck; or some combination. For further discussion of the 2009 test, see CRS Report R41160, *North Korea's 2009 Nuclear Test: Containment, Monitoring, Implications*, by Jonathan E. Medalia.

In response to the event, the U.N. Security Council adopted resolution 1874 on June 12, 2009.[92] Among other things, the resolution "express[es] the gravest concern" at the nuclear test, "condemns in the strongest terms the nuclear test," calls for inspection of cargo to and from North Korea under certain circumstances and conditions, and provides for various financial sanctions. (See CRS Report R40684, *North Korea's Second Nuclear Test: Implications of U.N. Security Council Resolution 1874*, coordinated by Mary Beth D. Nikitin and Mark E. Manyin.)

The February 2013 Nuclear Test

Since shortly after the second test, there were conflicting, ambiguous, or speculative reports on whether North Korea was preparing for another nuclear test, with some as recent as late 2012.[93]

(...continued)

%20Won_Young_Kim%20_Paul_Richards%20and%20Lynn_Sykes.pdf.

[91] Comprehensive Nuclear-Test-Ban Treaty Organization Preparatory Commission, "Experts Sure about the Nature of the DPRK Event," (referring to the May 2009 North Korean test), June 12, 2009, http://www.ctbto.org/press-centre/highlights/2009/experts-sure-about-nature-of-the-dprk-event/. The International Monitoring System is a system to detect nuclear explosions worldwide. It is being built up by the Comprehensive Nuclear-Test-Ban Treaty Organization Preparatory Commission. See http://www.ctbto.org/verification-regime/.

[92] United Nations. Security Council. Resolution 1874 (2009) adopted by the Security Council at its 6141st meeting, on 12 June 2009, S/Res/1874 (2009), http://daccess-dds-ny.un.org/doc/UNDOC/GEN/N09/368/49/PDF/N0936849.pdf?OpenElement.

[93] See, for example, David Chance, "For North Korea, Next Step Is a Nuclear Test," Reuters, December 13, 2012, http://www.reuters.com/article/2012/12/13/us-korea-north-rocket-idUSBRE8BB02K20121213; "Ex-USFK [U.S. Forces Korea] Commander Warns Against North's Nuclear and Missile Threats," *Korea Times,* September 13, 2012, http://www.koreatimes.co kr/www/news/nation/2012/09/205_119828 html; and Foster Klug and Matthew Pennington, "Photos Show NKorea Nuclear Readiness," Associated Press/ABC News, December 28, 2012, http://abcnews.go.com/International/wireStory/ap-exclusive-photos-show-nkorea-nuclear-readiness-18079671.

In early 2013 North Korea announced that it would conduct another nuclear test, and it did so on February 12, 2013. Reuters quoted North Korea's state-run Korean Central News Agency as saying, "It was confirmed that the nuclear test that was carried out at a high level in a safe and perfect manner using a miniaturized and lighter nuclear device with greater explosive force than previously did not pose any negative impact on the surrounding ecological environment."[94]

The Office of the Director of National Intelligence issued the following statement: "The U.S. Intelligence Community assesses that North Korea probably conducted an underground nuclear explosion in the vicinity of P'unggye on February 12, 2013. The explosion yield was approximately several kilotons. Analysis of the event continues."[95] The U.S. Geologic Survey stated that the test had a seismic magnitude of 5.1.[96] The Preparatory Commission for the Comprehensive Nuclear-Test-Ban Treaty Organization (CTBTO) operates the International Monitoring System (IMS, described in more detail below), which consists of a global network of seismographs and other instruments to detect nuclear tests, laboratories to analyze certain types of data, and an International Data Center (IDC) to further analyze data and disseminate the results.[97] On February 12, CTBTO stated, "The CTBTO's first and preliminary automatic detections were made by up to 25 seismic stations around the world. The first data were made available to CTBTO Member States in little more than one hour, and before the DPRK's announcement. The event measured 5.0 in magnitude, which is around twice as large as the DPRK's nuclear test in 2009 (4.52) and much larger than the one in 2006 (4.1)."[98] (Seismic magnitude is measured on a logarithmic scale; a magnitude 5 event is 10 times as large as a magnitude 4 event.) Seismic magnitude is an approximate measure of yield, as the magnitude detected at an individual seismic station can be affected by the type of rock or soil in which the test is conducted; whether the rock or soil is wet or dry (rock or soil saturated with water transmits a seismic signal more efficiently); whether the test device was packed tightly into the rock or soil, which would transmit seismic waves more efficiently, or placed in a large cavity, which would muffle the signal; the types and locations of rock formations between the test site and the seismic station; and so on. By February 15, 96 IMS stations had sent data to the IDC.[99]

Since many IMS seismic stations detected the test, the CTBTO had ample data for estimating the location of the test, placing it near North Korea's previous tests. The data also permitted estimating the depth of the test. Seismic signals originating deep in the earth indicate that the

---

[94] Jack Kim, "North Korea Confirms 'Successful' Nuclear Test: KCNA," Reuters, February 12, 2013.

[95] Office of the Director of National Intelligence, *Statement by the Office of the Director of National Intelligence on North Korea's Declared Nuclear Test on February 12, 2013*, February 12, 2013, http://www.dni.gov/index.php/ newsroom/press-releases/191-press-releases-2013/809-statement-by-the-office-of-the-director-of-national-intelligence-on-north-korea's.

[96] U.S. Geologic Survey, *Poster of the North Korea Seismic Event of 12 February 2013 - Magnitude 5.1*, February 12, 2013, http://earthquake.usgs.gov/earthquakes/eqarchives/poster/2013/20130212.php.

[97] For information on this monitoring system, see Preparatory Commission for the Comprehensive Nuclear-Test-Ban Treaty Organization, "Verification Regime," http://www.ctbto.org/verification-regime/. Many other seismographs not part of the IMS can contribute data on seismic events. See, for example, Incorporated Research Institutions for Seismology, "Global Seismographic Network" (map), January 2013, http://www.iris.edu/hq/programs/gsn/maps. In addition, the United States and other nations have their own equipment for monitoring nuclear testing.

[98] Preparatory Commission for the Comprehensive Nuclear-Test-Ban Treaty Organization, *On the CTBTO's Detection in North Korea*, Vienna, Austria, February 12, 2013, http://www.ctbto.org/press-centre/press-releases/2013/on-the-ctbtos-detection-in-north-korea/.

[99] Preparatory Commission for the Comprehensive Nuclear-Test-Ban Treaty Organization, "Update on CTBTO Findings Related to the Announced Nuclear Test by North Korea," February 15, 2013, http://www.ctbto.org/press-centre/highlights/2013/update-on-ctbto-findings-related-to-the-announced-nuclear-test-by-north-korea/.

---

source was an earthquake; signals originating near the surface are consistent with either an earthquake or an explosion. The data indicated a shallow depth for the event.

A key question is whether the device used uranium or plutonium. Since it requires less plutonium than uranium to sustain a fission reaction, a nuclear weapon made using plutonium can be smaller and lighter than one made using uranium. A plutonium warhead could thus be more readily carried by a missile, or carried to a longer range, than a uranium warhead. However,

> it appears that plutonium is a dead end for Pyongyang's nuclear arsenal because it shut down and has not restarted its five megawatt electric plutonium production reactor. Although we have seen no direct evidence of a highly enriched uranium (HEU) production program in North Korea, judging from the available evidence, we think the next bomb test will be based on HEU, or multiple bombs will be tested simultaneously, using both HEU and plutonium.[100]

On the other hand, a report of June 2013 indicated that North Korea was in the process of restarting its plutonium reactor.[101]

If certain radioactive gases leak from the test quickly, are collected quickly by ground- or air-based equipment, and are analyzed quickly, it may be possible to determine whether the device used uranium or plutonium. This sequence must be performed within hours because, after that time, radioactive decay prevents differentiating between the two materials. Even if such rapid action is not possible, certain radioactive gases released from the test can travel thousands of miles and can be analyzed by the IMS to confirm that an explosion is nuclear. This was done for the 2006 test but not for the 2009 test, as the latter apparently did not vent radioactive material.

If particles of debris from the device vent into the atmosphere and are collected by equipment operated by the IMS, the United States, or others, analysis of the debris can reveal considerable information about the device, including whether it contained uranium or plutonium.[102] The IMS, for example, has three ground stations within 1,000 miles of the test site that can collect radionuclides from the test,[103] and the United States reportedly sent aircraft equipped with sensors in an effort to collect such material.[104] Whether the absence of venting in the 2009 test was due to more careful sealing of the test shaft, better knowledge of test site geology, deeper burial of the test device, luck, or some combination is not known; North Korea's success in preventing venting in 2009 plus additional study might make venting unlikely for the 2013 test. The 2013 test apparently was of higher yield than the 2009 test, though the effect of somewhat higher yield on venting is unclear; some argue that venting is more likely for a very low yield test because there is less energy to melt rock, sealing the test cavity. Thorough analysis of debris collected, if any, may take days or weeks. On February 15, the CTBTO stated that there were no signs of

---

[100] Frank Pabian and Siegfried Hecker, "Contemplating a Third Nuclear Test in North Korea," *Bulletin of the Atomic Scientists* (online edition), August 6, 2012.

[101] "Update on Yongbyon: Restart of Plutonium Production Reactor Nears Completion; Work Continues on the Experimental Light Water Reactor," by Jeffrey Lewis and Nick Hansen, *38 North*, June 3, 2013, http://38north.org/2013/06/yongbyon060313/.

[102] The United States obtained such information by analyzing debris from the Soviet Union's first atomic bomb test in 1949 and its first hydrogen bomb test in 1953. Richard Rhodes, *Dark Sun: The Making of the Hydrogen Bomb* (New York: Simon & Schuster, 1995), pp. 371-372, 524-525.

[103] For a map of IMS stations, go to http://www.ctbto.org/map/ and click on "International Monitoring System."

[104] David Sanger and Choe Sang-Hun, "North Korea Confirms It Conducted 3d Nuclear Test," *New York Times* (online edition), February 12, 2013.

radioactive release from the test, but that it was too soon to say whether the test had released any radioactive material.[105] However, between April 8 and 14, IMS stations detected radioactive isotopes of xenon consistent with a North Korean test of February 12.[106]

North Korea's nuclear program continues. Reports of 2014 indicate construction at the Yongbyon nuclear reactor site,[107] including construction of a new reactor at Yongbyon that may be able to produce enough plutonium for five to six warheads per year;[108] construction at the Sohae Satellite Launching Station;[109] and work to miniaturize nuclear warheads.[110] However, a report of August 2014 indicated, based on satellite imagery showing little activity at the test site at Punggye-ri, that another nuclear test did not appear imminent.[111]

For additional information on North Korea's nuclear weapons program, see CRS Report RL34256, *North Korea's Nuclear Weapons: Technical Issues*, by Mary Beth D. Nikitin. For information on systems and technology for monitoring nuclear tests, see CRS Report R41160, *North Korea's 2009 Nuclear Test: Containment, Monitoring, Implications*, by Jonathan E. Medalia.

As of September 2014, North Korea had not signed the CTBT.

CTBT Negotiations, Provisions, Entry into Force; CTBTO Budget

CTBT Negotiations and the Nuclear Nonproliferation Treaty

The Conference on Disarmament, or CD, calls itself "the sole multilateral disarmament negotiating forum of the international community." It is affiliated with, funded by, but

---

[105] Personal communication from Comprehensive Nuclear-Test-Ban Treaty Preparatory Commission, February 15, 2013.

[106] Comprehensive Nuclear-Test-Ban Treaty Organization Preparatory Commission, "CTBTO detects radioactivity consistent with 12 February announced North Korean nuclear test," press release, April 23, 2013, http://www.ctbto.org/press-centre/press-releases/2013/ctbto-detects-radioactivity-consistent-with-12-february-announced-north-korean-nuclear-test/, and accompanying the foregoing source, Comprehensive Nuclear-Test-Ban Treaty Organization Preparatory Commission, "Media questions / answers on radionuclide detection," http://www.ctbto.org/the-treaty/developments-after-1996/2013-dprk-announced-nuclear-test/media-questions-answers-on-radionuclide-detection/.

[107] David Albright, Serena Kelleher-Vergantini, William Baker, and Won Gi You, "Activities Detected at North Korea's Yongbyon Nuclear Site," Institute for Science and International Security, August 6, 2014, http://www.isis-online.org/uploads/isis-reports/documents/Yongbyon_August_6_FINAL.pdf.

[108] "New Reactor May Boost North Korea's Warhead Production: Expert," Global Security Newswire, July 7, 2014, http://www.nti.org/gsn/article/expert-says-pyongyangs-fissile-material-production-capacity-could-rise-sharply-new-reactor/.

[109] Nick Hansen, "North Korea's Sohae Facility: Preparations for Future Large Rocket Launches Progresses; New Unidentified Buildings," 38 North, July 29, 2014, http://38north.org/2014/07/sohae073014/.

[110] Bruce Klingner, "Allies Should Confront Imminent North Korean Nuclear Threat," Heritage Foundation Backgrounder 2913, http://www.heritage.org/research/reports/2014/06/allies-should-confront-imminent-north-korean-nuclear-threat.

[111] Jack Liu, "North Korea's Punggye-ri Nuclear Test Site: All Quiet for the Moment," 38 North, August 11, 2014, http://38north.org/2014/08/punggye081114/.

---

autonomous from the United Nations. It operates by consensus; each member state can block a decision. On August 10, 1993, the CD gave its Ad Hoc Committee on a Nuclear Test Ban "a mandate to negotiate a CTB." On November 19, 1993, the United Nations General Assembly unanimously approved a resolution calling for negotiation of a CTBT. The CD's 1994 session opened in Geneva on January 25, with negotiation of a CTBT its top priority.

The priority had to do with extension of the Nuclear Non-Proliferation Treaty (NPT).[112] That treaty entered into force in 1970. It divided the world into nuclear "haves"—the United States, Soviet Union, Britain, France, and China, the five[113] declared nuclear powers, which are also the permanent five ("P5") members of the U.N. Security Council—and nuclear "have-nots." The P5 would be the only States Party to the NPT to have nuclear weapons, but they (and others) would negotiate in good faith on halting the nuclear arms race soon, on nuclear disarmament, and on general and complete disarmament. Nonnuclear weapon states saw attainment of a CTBT as the touchstone of good faith on these matters. The NPT provided for reviews every five years; a review in 1995, 25 years after it entered into force, would determine whether to extend the treaty indefinitely or for one or more fixed periods. The Review and Extension Conference of April-May 1995 extended the treaty indefinitely. Extension was accompanied by certain measures, including a Decision on Principles and Objectives for Nuclear Non-Proliferation and Disarmament that set forth goals on universality of the NPT, nuclear weapon free zones, etc., and stressed the importance of completing "the negotiations on a universal and internationally and effectively verifiable Comprehensive Nuclear-Test-Ban Treaty no later than 1996."

The extension decision, binding on States Party to the NPT, was contentious. Nonnuclear States Party argued that the P5 failed to meet their NPT obligations by not concluding a CTBT. They saw progress on winding down the arms race as inadequate. They assailed the NPT as discriminatory because it divides the world into nuclear and nonnuclear states, and argued for a regime in which no nation has nuclear weapons. The CTBT, in their view, symbolized this regime because, unlike the NPT, the P5 would give up something tangible, the ability to develop new sophisticated warheads. Some nonnuclear states saw NPT extension as their last source of leverage for a CTBT. Other nonnuclear states felt that the NPT was in the interests of all but would-be proliferators, that anything less than indefinite extension would undermine the security of most nations, and that the NPT was too important to put at risk as a means of pressuring the P5 for a CTBT. The explicit linkage finally drawn between CTBT and NPT lent urgency to negotiations on the former.

The CD reached a draft treaty in August 1996. India argued that the CTBT "should be securely anchored in the global disarmament context and be linked through treaty language to the elimination of all nuclear weapons in a time bound framework."[114] India also wanted a treaty to bar weapons research not involving nuclear tests. The draft treaty did not meet these conditions, which the nuclear weapon states rejected, so India vetoed it at the CD on August 20, barring it from going to the U.N. General Assembly as a CD document. As an alternate way to open the

---

[112] For text of the treaty, see http://www.state.gov/t/isn/trty/16281 htm#treaty.

[113] For detailed information on the CTBT negotiations, see Jaap Ramaker, Jenifer Mackby, Peter Marshall, and Robert Geil, *The Final Test: A History of the Comprehensive Nuclear-Test-Ban Treaty Negotiations,* Vienna, Austria, Provisional Technical Secretariat of the Preparatory Commission for the Comprehensive Nuclear-Test-Ban Treaty Organization, 2003, 291 p.

[114] India. Embassy. "Statement by Ms. Arundhati Ghose, Ambassador/Permanent Representative of India to UN, Geneva, in the Plenary of the Conference on Disarmament on January 25, 1996," at http://www.indianembassy.org/policy/Disarmament/cd(jan2596) htm.

treaty for signing, Australia on August 23 asked the General Assembly to consider a resolution to adopt the draft CTBT text and for the Secretary-General to open it for signing so it could be adopted by a simple majority, or by the two-thirds majority that India sought, avoiding the need for consensus. A potential pitfall was that the resolution (the treaty text) was subject to amendment, yet the nuclear weapon states viewed amendments as unacceptable. India did not raise obstacles to the vote, which was held September 10, with 158 nations in favor, 3 against (India, Bhutan, and Libya), 5 abstentions, and 19 not voting.

A sixth five-year NPT review conference was held April 24-May 19, 2000, in New York. U.S. rejection of the CTBT, lack of Chinese ratification, U.S. efforts to seek renegotiation of the ABM Treaty, and efforts to ban nuclear weapons in the Middle East led some to fear a dire outcome of the conference. However, some contentious issues were ironed out or avoided, and concessions were made. For example, a joint statement by the P5 to the conference on May 1 said, "No efforts should be spared to make sure that the CTBT is a universal and internationally and effectively verifiable treaty and to secure its earliest entry into force."[115] As a result of effort by many nations, the final document of the conference was adopted by consensus. The document included a 13-step Nuclear Disarmament Plan of Action, the first two elements of which called for the early entry into force of the treaty and a moratorium on nuclear explosions pending entry into force.

At the NPT Review Conference of May 2005, the CTBT was a point of contention. For example, Alberto Romulo, Secretary of Foreign Affairs, Republic of the Philippines, said, "Plans to develop new nuclear weapons technology and failure to bring the Comprehensive Test Ban Treaty (CTBT) into force seriously erode the historic foundations of the NPT."[116] Ihor Dolhov, Deputy Foreign Minister for Foreign Affairs of Ukraine, said, "Ukraine continues to underscore the importance and urgency of an early entry into force of the Treaty and calls upon all States who have not yet done so to adhere to the Treaty without delay and unconditionally."[117] Ambassador Ronaldo Sardenberg of Brazil said, "Brazil has consistently called for the universalization of the CTBT, which we consider to be an essential element of the disarmament and non-proliferation regime."[118]

The eighth NPT review conference was held May 3-28, 2010, at U.N. headquarters in New York. Many speakers supported the CTBT. Secretary of State Clinton said, "We have made a commitment to ratify the Comprehensive Test Ban Treaty."[119] Indonesia's Minister for Foreign

---

[115] France. Embassy of France in the United States. "2000 Review Conference of the Parties to the Treaty on the Non-Proliferation of Nuclear Weapons: Statement by the Delegations of France, The People's Republic of China, The Russian Federation, The United Kingdom of Great Britain and Northern Ireland and The United States of America," New York, May 1, 2000, at http://www.ambafrance-us.org/news/statmnts/2000/tnp5.asp.

[116] Philippines. Mission to the United Nations. "Collective Action: Regional Responsibility and Global Accountability Towards a World Free of Nuclear Weapons, Statement by H.E. Dr. Alberto G. Romulo, Secretary of Foreign Affairs, Republic of the Philippines, at the General Debate of the 2005 Review Conference of the Nuclear Non-Proliferation Treaty, New York, 11 May 2005," p. 2, at http://www.un.org/events/npt2005/statements/npt11philippines.pdf.

[117] Ukraine. Permanent Mission of Ukraine to the United Nations. "Statement by H.E. Mr. Ihor Dolhov, Deputy Minister for Foreign Affairs of Ukraine, at the 2005 NPT Review Conference, New York, 5 May 2005," p. 4, at http://www.un.org/events/npt2005/statements/npt05ukraine.pdf.

[118] Brazil. "VII Review Conference of Treaty on the Non-Proliferation of Nuclear Weapons, Statement by the Head of the Delegation of Brazil, Ambassador Ronaldo Sardenberg, New York, 2 May 2005," p. 4, at http://www.un.org/events/npt2005/statements/npt04brazil.pdf.

[119] The Delegation of the United States of America to the 2010 Review Conference of the Treaty on the Non-Proliferation of Nuclear Weapons, 3-28 May 2010, "Statement by Secretary of State Hillary Rodham Clinton to the (continued...)

Affairs, R.M. Marty M. Natalegawa, announced, "Indonesia is initiating the process of the ratification of the Comprehensive Nuclear Test Ban Treaty."[120] Indonesia is one of the remaining nine nations that must ratify the CTBT for it to enter into force. (Indonesia subsequently deposited its instruments of ratification with the United Nations on February 6, 2012,[121] reducing to eight the number of nations that must ratify the treaty for it to enter into force.) Natalegawa, in a separate statement on behalf of the Non-Aligned Movement (NAM), said, "The NAM States Parties [to the NPT] strongly urge this Review Conference to clearly and categorically reject the policies of nuclear deterrence and place a ban on all forms of nuclear weapon testing with a view to their total elimination."[122] A speaker representing the European Union identified "achieving rapid entry into force of the CTBT" as an "indispensable [step] towards fulfillment of the obligations and final objective enshrined in Article VI of the NPT."[123] The five original nuclear weapon states declared,

> We reaffirm our determination to abide by our respective moratoria on nuclear test explosions before entry into force of the Comprehensive Nuclear-Test-Ban Treaty (CTBT) and call on all States to refrain from conducting a nuclear test explosion. The moratoria, though important, are not a substitute for legally binding commitments under the CTBT. We will continue our efforts aimed at early entry into force of the CTBT and achieving its universality and call upon all States that have not yet done so to sign and ratify this Treaty.[124]

In its final document, "the Conference reaffirms the vital importance of the entry into force of the Comprehensive Nuclear-Test-Ban Treaty as a core element of the international nuclear disarmament and non-proliferation regime," and resolved that "all nuclear-weapon States undertake to ratify the Comprehensive Nuclear-Test-Ban Treaty with all expediency."[125]

The next (ninth) NPT Review Conference is scheduled for 2015. Several preparatory committee sessions are held prior to each review conference. The first session for the ninth review

---

(...continued)

2010 Review Conference of the Treaty on the Non-Proliferation of Nuclear Weapons," general debate, New York, May 3, 2010, p. 6, http://www.un.org/en/conf/npt/2010/statements/pdf/usa_en.pdf.

[120] Republic of Indonesia. Permanent Mission of the Republic of Indonesia to the United Nations. "Statement by H.E. Dr. R.M. Marty M. Natalegawa, Minister for Foreign Affairs of the Republic of Indonesia at the General Debate of the 2010 NPT Review Conference," New York, May 3, 2010, p. 2, http://www.un.org/en/conf/npt/2010/statements/pdf/indonesia_en.pdf.

[121] United Nations Office for Disarmament Affairs. "Indonesia Deposits Instrument of Ratification to the Comprehensive Nuclear-Test-Ban Treaty," February 6, 2012, http://www.un.org/disarmament/content/news/indonesia_ctbt/.

[122] "Statement by H.E. Dr. R.M. Marty M. Natalegawa, Minister for Foreign Affairs of the Republic of Indonesia, on Behalf of the NAM States Party to the Non-Proliferation of Nuclear Weapons Treaty (NPT), before the 2010 Review Conference of the Parties to the Non-Proliferation of Nuclear Weapons Treaty," May 3, 2010, p. 3, http://www.un.org/en/conf/npt/2010/statements/pdf/nam_en.pdf.

[123] "Statement on Behalf of the European Union by H.E. Catherine Ashton, High Representative of the European Union for Foreign Affairs and Security Policy at the General Debate of the Review Conference of the Treaty on the Non-Proliferation of Nuclear Weapons (NPT)," United Nations, New York, May 3, 2010, p. 5, http://www.un.org/en/conf/npt/2010/statements/pdf/eu_en.pdf.

[124] "Statement by the People's Republic of China, France, the Russian Federation, the United Kingdom of Great Britain and Northern Ireland, and the United States of America to the 2010 Non-Proliferation Treaty Review Conference," May 5, 2010, p. 2, http://www.un.org/en/conf/npt/2010/statements/pdf/russia5_en.pdf.

[125] 2010 Review Conference of the Parties to the Treaty on the Non-Proliferation of Nuclear Weapons, *Final Document,* Volume I, NPT/CONF010/50 (Vol. I), p. 22, http://www.un.org/ga/search/view_doc.asp?symbol=NPT/CONF.2010/50%20(VOL.I).

---

conference was held April 30-May 11, 2012, in Vienna; the second session was held April 22-May 3, 2013, in Geneva, and the third session was held April 28-May 9, 2014, in New York.[126] Among other things, delegates called for entry into force of the CTBT and referenced the final document of the 2010 review conference. In particular, a working paper submitted to the 2012 session stated,

> The Vienna Group of Ten firmly believes that the Comprehensive Nuclear-Test-Ban Treaty constitutes an effective measure of nuclear disarmament and nuclear non-proliferation in all its aspects and is vital to the Treaty on the Non-Proliferation of Nuclear Weapons. The Test-Ban Treaty was an integral part of the 1995 decision to indefinitely extend the Non-Proliferation Treaty. The Group therefore stresses that the entry into force of the Test-Ban Treaty is of the utmost urgency and recalls that the 2000 and 2010 Review Conferences of the Parties to the Non-Proliferation Treaty reaffirmed the vital importance of the entry into force of the Test-Ban Treaty, with the action plan from the 2010 Review Conference again emphasizing the resolve of States parties to the Non-Proliferation Treaty to achieve that aim. The Group reaffirms that the provisions of article V of the Non-Proliferation Treaty are to be interpreted in the light of the Test-Ban Treaty.[127]

Key Provisions of the CTBT

Scope (Article I): The heart of the treaty is the obligation "not to carry out any nuclear weapon test explosion or any other nuclear explosion." This formulation bars even very low yield tests that some in the nuclear weapon states had wanted, and bars peaceful nuclear explosions that China had wanted, but rejects India's concern that a CTBT should "leave no loophole for activity, either explosive based or non-explosive based, aimed at the continued development and refinement of nuclear weapons."[128] Views differ on whether the ban covers tests with the tiniest nuclear yield. Opponents of the treaty argue that the treaty "fails to define what it purports to prohibit," that is, a "nuclear test," that Russia considers hydronuclear tests (those producing grams to hundreds of pounds of nuclear yield) as permissible, and that Russia has conducted such tests. Further, it is argued, tests with very low nuclear yields could not be detected using current technologies.[129] Supporters respond that the negotiating record makes clear that Russia agreed that "experiments which do produce a nuclear yield ... would be banned."[130] According to the State Department, the CTBT

---

[126] The website "NPT Review Conferences and Preparatory Committees" of the United Nations Office for Disarmament Affairs, http://www.un.org/disarmament/WMD/Nuclear/NPT_Review_Conferences.shtml, has links to the preparatory committee meetings; these links, in turn, have links to documents from each meeting, including speeches by representatives of nations and groups of nations.

[127] Preparatory Committee for the 2015 Review Conference of the Parties to the Treaty on the Non-Proliferation of Nuclear Weapons, "Comprehensive Nuclear-Test-Ban Treaty," Working paper submitted by Australia, Austria, Canada, Denmark, Finland, Hungary, Ireland, the Netherlands, New Zealand, Norway and Sweden (the Vienna Group of Ten), March 16, 2012, NPT/CONF.2015/PC.I/WP.4, http://www.un.org/ga/search/view_doc.asp?symbol=NPT/CONF.2015/1.

[128] India, "Statement by Ms. Arundhati Ghose, ... January 25, 1996."

[129] Kathleen Bailey and Thomas Scheber, *The Comprehensive Test Ban Treaty: An Assessment of the Benefits, Costs, and Risks*, National Institute for Public Policy, March 2011, pp. 15-16.

[130] U.S. Congress, Senate Committee on Foreign Relations, *Final Review of the Comprehensive Nuclear Test Ban Treaty*, Hearing on Treaty Doc. 105-28, 106th Cong., 1st sess., October 7, 1999, S.Hrg. 106-262 (Washington: GPO, 2000), pp. 16-17, testimony of Stephen Ledogar, former chief negotiator of the Comprehensive Test Ban Treaty.

---

prohibits all nuclear explosions that produce a self-sustaining, supercritical chain reaction of any kind ... The decision not to include a specific definition of scope in the Treaty was a deliberate decision by the negotiating parties, including the United States, made to ensure that no loopholes were created by including a highly technical and specific list of what specific activities were and were not permitted under the Treaty. A thorough review of the history of the Treaty negotiation process, as well as statements by world leaders and the negotiators of the agreement, shows that all states understand and accept the CTBT as a "zero-yield" treaty.[131]

Organization (Article II): The treaty establishes a Comprehensive Nuclear-Test-Ban Treaty Organization (CTBTO), composed of all member states, to implement the treaty.[132] Three groups are under the CTBTO. The Conference of States Parties, composed of a representative from each member state, shall meet in annual and special sessions to consider and decide issues within the scope of the treaty and oversee the work of the other groups. An Executive Council with 51 member states shall, among other things, take action on requests for on-site inspection, and may request a special session of the Conference. A Technical Secretariat shall carry out verification functions, including operating an International Data Center (IDC), processing and reporting on data from an International Monitoring System, and receiving and processing requests for on-site inspections.

Verification (Article IV): The treaty establishes a verification regime. It provides for collection and dissemination of information, permits States Party to use national technical means of verification, and specifies verification responsibilities of the Technical Secretariat. It establishes an International Monitoring System (IMS) and provides for on-site inspections. The treaty calls for the IMS to have, when complete, 321 stations worldwide to monitor for signals that might indicate a nuclear explosion: 170 seismic stations to monitor seismic waves in the Earth; 11 hydroacoustic stations to monitor underwater sound waves; 60 arrays of infrasound detectors to monitor very low frequency sound waves in the atmosphere; and 80 radionuclide stations to detect radioactive particles and (for half the stations) radioactive xenon gas that a nuclear explosion might produce, as well as 16 radionuclide laboratories to analyze radioactive samples. Of the seismic stations, 50 are to be primary stations to provide data to IDC continuously and in real time, while 120 are to be auxiliary stations to provide data when requested by the IDC. As of September 2014, of the 337 facilities, 19 were planned, 19 were under construction, 21 were installed but not yet certified, and 278 had been certified, that is, they were completed and met the technical requirements of the Preparatory Commission.[133] Certified stations transmit data automatically and continuously to the IDC, excepting for the auxiliary stations and the radionuclide laboratories, which transmit data as requested by the IDC.[134] In March 2008, the Preparatory Commission launched the International Scientific Studies (ISS) Project. A conference to report the results was held in Vienna, Austria, on June 10-12, 2009.[135] "The ISS aim is to foster the CTBTO Preparatory Commission's ability to keep pace with scientific and technological

---

[131] U.S. Department of State. "Scope of the CTBT," fact sheet, 1 p., September 29, 2011, http://www.state.gov/t/avc/rls/173944 htm.

[132] For further information on the CTBTO, see its website at http://www.ctbto.org.

[133] The CTBTO Preparatory Commission provides updated information on the status of these facilities on its home page, http://www.ctbto.org/.

[134] Information provided by Annika Thunborg, Chief, Public Information, Comprehensive Nuclear-Test-Ban Treaty Preparatory Commission, personal communication, November 26, 2007.

[135] For links to publications of the conference, see "ISS09, International Scientific Studies," http://www.ctbto.org/specials/the-international-scientific-studies-project-iss/.

progress and to strengthen cooperation between the organization and the scientific community."[136] Critics would note that a focus on progress implies less focus on possible difficulties. The second conference in this series was held June 8-10, 2011, and the third was held June 17-21, 2013, both in Vienna.[137] In September 2008, the PrepCom conducted its large-scale Integrated Field Exercise 2008 in Kazakhstan to simulate a complete on-site inspection.[138] The PrepCom called the exercise a success.[139] In November 2010, the PrepCom held a simulated on-site inspection in Jordan to improve capability to detect evidence of clandestine testing.[140] [141] On October 24, 2011, the PrepCom endorsed a budget of $10.3 million for an integrated field exercise in 2014.[142] This exercise, to be held in Jordan in late 2014, is intended to "to simulate an almost entire on-site inspection ... the inspection team will conduct a meticulous search of a clearly defined inspection area to establish whether or not a nuclear explosion has been conducted. The exercise will be in response to a technically realistic and stimulating but fictional scenario."[143]

Review of the Treaty (Article VIII): The treaty provides for a conference 10 years after entry into force (unless a majority of States Party decide not to hold such a conference) to review the treaty's operation and effectiveness. Further review conferences may be held at subsequent intervals of 10 years or less. The treaty had not entered into force as of August 2014, so no Article VIII conference has been held.

Duration and Withdrawal (Article IX): "This treaty shall be of unlimited duration." However, "Each State Party shall, in exercising its national sovereignty, have the right to withdraw from this Treaty if it decides that extraordinary events related to the subject matter of this Treaty have jeopardized its supreme interests." President Clinton indicated his possible willingness to withdraw from the Treaty using this withdrawal provision, which is common to many arms control agreements, in his speech of August 11, 1995, discussed below, as one of several conditions under which the United States would enter the CTBT.

---

[136] ISS09—International Scientific Studies, "International Scientific Studies Conference, Vienna, 10-12 June 2009," p. 1.

[137] Documents from, and about, these conferences are available on the CTBTO Preparatory Commission website at http://www.ctbto.org/the-organization/science-and-technology-the-conference-series/.

[138] Preparatory Commission for the Comprehensive Nuclear-Test-Ban Treaty Organization, "CTBTO Inspectors Implement On-site Inspection Test Scenario in Kazakh Steppe," press release, September 12, 2008, at http://www.ctbto.org/press-centre/highlights/2008/ctbto-inspectors-implement-on-siteinspection-test-scenario-in-kazakh-steppe/12-september-2008-page-1/.

[139] Preparatory Commission for the Comprehensive Nuclear-Test-Ban Treaty, "Integrated Field Exercise 2008 Concludes Successfully," http://www.ctbto.org/press-centre/highlights/2008/integrated-field-exercise-2008concludes-successfully/8-october-2008-page-1/.

[140] Preparatory Commission for the Comprehensive Nuclear-Test-Ban Treaty, "Exercise to Inspect a Simulated Nuclear Test Site—Jordan, 1 to 12 November 2010," press release, November 1, 2010, http://www.ctbto.org/press-centre/press-releases/2010/exercise-to-inspect-a-simulated-nuclear-test-site-jordan-1-to-12-november-2010/.

[141] For a detailed technical discussion of CTBT monitoring and verification, see Ola Dahlman, Jenifer Mackby, Svein Mykkeltveit, and Hein Haak, *Detect and Deter: Can Countries Verify the Nuclear Test Ban?*, Dordrecht, Netherlands, Springer, 2011. For a countervailing view, see Kathleen Bailey and Thomas Scheber, *The Comprehensive Test Ban Treaty: An Assessment of the Benefits, Costs, and Risks*, Fairfax, VA, National Institute Press, 2011, pp. 17-23.

[142] Preparatory Commission for the Comprehensive Nuclear-Test-Ban Treaty Organization, "CTBTO Member States Take Test-Ban Verification to the Next Level," press release, October 24, 2011, http://www.ctbto.org/press-centre/press-releases/2011/ctbto-member-states-take-test-ban-verification-to-the-next-level/.

[143] "IFE14," http://www.ctbto.org/specials/integrated-field-exercise-2014/.

Entry Into Force (Article XIV): The treaty shall enter into force 180 days after 44 states named in Annex 2 have deposited instruments of ratification, but not less than two years after the treaty is opened for signature. The 44 states are those with nuclear reactors that participated in the work of the CD's 1996 session and were CD members as of June 18, 1996. This formulation includes nuclear-capable states and nuclear threshold states (in particular Israel, which, along with other States, joined the CD on June 17, 1996), and excludes the former Yugoslavia. Of the 44, as of September 2014, India, North Korea, and Pakistan had not signed the treaty and China, Egypt, Iran, Israel, and the United States had signed but not ratified it.

If the treaty has not entered into force three years after being opened for signature, and if a majority of states that have deposited instruments of ratification so desire, a conference of these states shall be held to decide how to accelerate ratification. Unless otherwise decided, subsequent conferences of this type shall be held annually until entry into force occurs. In practice, these conferences (often called Article XIV conferences) have been held every second year beginning in 1999. The CTBTO PrepCom serves as the secretariat of these conferences.

In a message to the third conference, in 2003, U.N. Secretary-General Kofi Annan urged the nations that had to ratify the treaty for it to enter into force, and especially North Korea, to ratify, and urged continuing the moratorium: "No nuclear testing must be tolerated under any circumstances."[144]

The sixth Article XIV conference was held September 24-25, 2009, at U.N. headquarters in New York; Secretary of State Hillary Rodham Clinton, among others, delivered remarks at the conference. The final declaration of the 2009 conference stated, "Relevant international developments since the 2007 Conference on Facilitating the Entry into Force of the CTBT make entry into force of the Treaty more urgent today than ever before," and adopted 10 measures to promote entry into force.[145]

The seventh conference was held September 23, 2011, at U.N. headquarters in New York. At this conference, Ellen Tauscher, Under Secretary of State for Arms Control and International Security, said that one of the highest priorities of the Obama Administration is ratification and entry into force of the treaty, that the United States was providing $34.4 million to the Comprehensive Nuclear-Test-Ban Treaty Organization Preparatory Commission beyond the assessed contribution, and that "we have begun the process of engaging the Senate," though with "no set timeframes."[146] The final declaration of the 2011 conference emphasized the importance of early entry into force of the treaty, called the ending of nuclear weapons testing "a meaningful step in the realization of the goal of eliminating nuclear weapons globally," and set forth 10 "concrete steps towards early entry into force," including encouraging the organization of regional seminars to increase awareness of the importance of the treaty, providing states with legal assistance regarding the

---

[144] U.N. "No Nuclear Testing Must Be Tolerated under Any Circumstances." Press Release SG/SM/8843, DC/2885, September 3, 2003, at http://www.un.org/News/Press/docs/2003/sgsm8843.doc.htm.

[145] "Annex: Final Declaration and Measures to Promote the Entry into Force of the Comprehensive Nuclear-Test-Ban Treaty," in Conference on Facilitating the Entry into Force of the Comprehensive Nuclear-Test-Ban Treaty, New York, 24-25 September 2009, "Report of the Conference," CTBT-Art. XIV/2009/6, October 8, 2009, http://www.ctbto.org/fileadmin/user_upload/Art_14_2009/CTBT-Art.XIV-2009-6.pdf.

[146] U.S. Department of State. Ellen Tauscher, Under Secretary for Arms Control and International Security, remarks at CTBT Article XIV Conference, New York, NY, September 23, 2011.

ratification process, and encouraging cooperation with intergovernmental organizations, nongovernmental organizations, and others to raise awareness of and support for the treaty.[147]

The eighth conference was held September 27, 2013, at U.N. Headquarters in New York.[148] The final declaration "affirm[ed] the importance and urgency of achieving early entry into force of the Treaty as a crucial practical step for systematic and progressive efforts towards nuclear disarmament and nuclear non-proliferation," "reaffirm[ed] our strong belief that it is essential to maintain momentum in building all elements of the verification regime, which will be capable of verifying compliance with the Treaty at its entry into force," and adopted 11 "concrete steps towards early entry into force and universalization of the Treaty."[149] It called upon the eight states whose ratification is necessary for the CTBT to enter into force to ratify the treaty "at the earliest possible date."[150]

Annexes: Annex 1 lists the regional groupings of states; Annex 2 lists the 44 states that must ratify the treaty, pursuant to Article XIV, for it to enter into force.

Protocol: The Protocol provides details on the IMS and on functions of the International Data Center (Part I); spells out on-site inspection procedures in great detail (Part II); and provides for certain confidence-building measures (Part III). Annex 1 to the Protocol lists International Monitoring System facilities: seismic stations, radionuclide stations and laboratories, hydroacoustic stations, and infrasound stations. Annex 2 to the Protocol provides a list of variables that, among others, may be used in analyzing data from these stations to screen for possible explosions.

International Efforts on Behalf of Entry into Force

Article II of the CTBT establishes the Comprehensive Nuclear-Test-Ban Treaty Organization (CTBTO). However, that organization will not come into existence until and unless the treaty enters into force. As an interim measure, on November 29, 1996, states that had signed the treaty adopted a resolution establishing the Preparatory Commission (PrepCom) for the CTBTO "for the purpose of carrying out the necessary preparations for the effective implementation of the Comprehensive Nuclear-Test-Ban Treaty, and for preparing for the first session of the Conference of the States Parties to that Treaty."[151] The PrepCom held 41 meetings from 1996 through 2013;

---

[147] Conference on Facilitating the Entry into Force of the Comprehensive Nuclear-Test-Ban Treaty, "Final Declaration and Measures to Promote the Entry into Force of the Comprehensive Nuclear-Test-Ban Treaty," New York, September 23, 2011, http://www.ctbto.org/fileadmin/user_upload/Art_14_2011/23-09-11/Final_Declaration.pdf.

[148] Conference on Facilitating the Entry into Force of the Comprehensive Nuclear-Test-Ban Treaty, 27 September 2013, United Nations, New York, USA, http://www.ctbto.org/the-treaty/article-xiv-conferences/2013-conference-on-facilitating-the-entry-into-force-of-the-comprehensive-nuclear-test-ban-treaty-united-nations-new-york-usa/. This website provides links to many documents from the conference.

[149] Conference on Facilitating the Entry into Force of the Comprehensive Nuclear-Test-Ban Treaty, New York, 27 September 2013, "Final Declaration and Measures to Promote the Entry into Force of the Comprehensive Nuclear-Test-Ban Treaty," http://www.ctbto.org/fileadmin/user_upload/Art_14_2013/Statements/Final_Declaration.pdf.

[150] Conference on Facilitating the Entry into Force of the Comprehensive Nuclear-Test-Ban Treaty, New York, 27 September 2013, "Final Declaration and Measures to Promote the Entry into Force of the Comprehensive Nuclear-Test-Ban Treaty," http://www.ctbto.org/fileadmin/user_upload/Art_14_2013/Statements/Final_Declaration.pdf.

[151] "Resolution Establishing the Preparatory Commission for the Comprehensive Nuclear Test-Ban Treaty Organization," Adopted by the States Signatories, November 19, 1996: "Annex—Text on the Establishment of a Preparatory Commission for the Comprehensive Nuclear Test-Ban Treaty Organization," paragraph 1, http://www.fas.org/nuke/control/ctbt/text/ctbt4.htm.

---

one for 2014 was held June 16-17, and another is scheduled for October 28-30. Eight meetings of working groups and advisory groups were held or are scheduled for 2014. The PrepCom also holds training sessions, workshops, etc.[152] Examples are "iTunes University," which enables users to download information from the CTBTO website, and the CTBT public policy course, "Verification Through Diplomacy and Science."[153] The CTBTO PrepCom also held a CTBT Science and Technology Conference from June 17 to 21, 2013.[154]

In addition to Article XIV conferences, there have been other calls for entry into force. For example, in September of years between Article XIV conferences, foreign ministers of nations that strongly support the CTBT meet on the margins of the U.N. General Assembly. According to the CTBTO PrepCom, "The aim of these meetings is to sustain and generate further political momentum as well as public attention for the entry into force of the Treaty. To that end, the Ministers adopt and sign Joint Ministerial Statements that are open for adherence by other countries."[155] At the first such meeting, in September 2002, a statement by 18 foreign ministers, including those of Britain, France, and Russia, called for early entry into force. There have also been U.N. resolutions on the CTBT. On November 22, 2002, the U.N. General Assembly adopted resolution 57/100 (164 for, 1 against [United States], 5 abstentions) urging states to maintain their nuclear test moratoria and urging states that had not signed and ratified the CTBT to do so as soon as possible and to avoid actions that would defeat its object and purpose. These and other efforts continue, as noted below.

A conference of the Non-Aligned Movement, which has 116 members, ended on February 25, 2003. Its Final Document stated that the heads of state or government "stressed the significance of achieving universal adherence to the Comprehensive Nuclear-Test-Ban Treaty (CTBT), including by all the Nuclear Weapons States."[156] On September 23, 2004, foreign ministers from 42 nations called for prompt ratification of the CTBT, especially by nations whose ratification is required for entry into force.[157] The Weapons of Mass Destruction Commission, an international commission organized by Sweden, issued a report in June 2006 that, among other things, urged all states that have not done so to sign and ratify the CTBT "unconditionally and without delay." It recommended that the 2007 conference of CTBT signatories "should address the possibility of a provisional entry into force of the treaty." It stated, "The Commission believes that a U.S. decision to ratify the CTBT would strongly influence other countries to follow suit. It would decisively improve the chances for entry into force of the treaty and would have more positive ramifications for arms control and disarmament than any other single measure."[158] In September 2006, to mark the 10th anniversary of the CTBT's opening for signature, 59 foreign ministers issued a joint statement on the treaty that "[calls] upon all States that have not yet done so to sign

---

[152] Preparatory Commission for the Comprehensive Nuclear-Test-Ban Treaty Organization, "Calendar of Events," http://www.ctbto.org/the-organization/calendar-of-events/.

[153] Preparatory Commission for the Comprehensive Nuclear-Test-Ban Treaty Organization, "CTBT Educational Resources," http://www.ctbto.org/specials/ctbt-educational-resources/.

[154] The conference website is http://www.ctbto.org/specials/snt2013/.

[155] Preparatory Commission for the Comprehensive Nuclear-Test-Ban Treaty Organization, "CTBT Ministerial Meetings," http://www.ctbto.org/the-treaty/ctbt-ministerial-meetings/.

[156] Non-Aligned Movement, Kuala Lumpur Summit, February 20-25, 2003, "Non-Aligned Movement Conference Stresses Importance of CTBT," at http://pws.ctbto.org/press_centre/featured_articles/250203_nam.html.

[157] Japan. Ministry of Foreign Affairs. "Joint Ministerial Statement on the CTBT," New York, September 23, 2004, http://www.mofa.go.jp/policy/un/disarmament/ctbt/joint0409.html.

[158] Weapons of Mass Destruction Commission, *Weapons of Terror: Freeing the World of Nuclear, Biological and Chemical Arms.* June 2006, p. 107, 108, at http://www.wmdcommission.org/files/Weapons_of_Terror.pdf.

---

and ratify the Treaty without delay, in particular those whose ratification is needed for its entry into force."[159]

In January 2007, George Shultz, William Perry, Henry Kissinger, and Sam Nunn urged the United States to work toward a world without nuclear weapons, with one step "Initiating a bipartisan process with the Senate, including understandings to increase confidence and provide for periodic review, to achieve ratification of the Comprehensive Test Ban Treaty, taking advantage of recent technical advances, and working to secure ratification by other key states."[160] In response, a few weeks later, Mikhail Gorbachev called on nuclear weapon states to ratify the CTBT, among other actions.[161] On November 19, former Secretary of Defense Harold Brown and former Director of Central Intelligence John Deutch suggested a five-year renewable CTBT in lieu of the current treaty.[162] In January 2008, Shultz, Perry, Kissinger, and Nunn renewed their call for, among other things, "a process for bringing the [CTBT] into effect" and called IMS "an effort the U.S. should urgently support even prior to [CTBT] ratification."[163] In Senate testimony of April 2008, Siegfried Hecker, former Director of Los Alamos National Laboratory, stated that without nuclear tests, "slowly our confidence [in U.S. nuclear weapons] zeroes," but that resumed U.S. testing runs the risk that other nations would resume testing. "And as I personally today weigh those risks, I definitely come out in favor that it's in our nation's and the world's interest to actually ratify the Comprehensive Test Ban Treaty."[164] On April 30, 2011, foreign ministers from 10 nations stated, "We call on all States which have not yet done so to sign and ratify the CTBT.... We believe that an effective end to nuclear testing will enhance and not weaken our national as well as global security and would significantly bolster the global non-proliferation and disarmament regime."[165] "To ensure an innovative and focused approach to advance the CTBT's ratification by the remaining Annex 2 States, a group comprising eminent personalities and internationally recognized experts was launched on 26 September 2013 at the United Nations Headquarters in New York."[166] This group issued a statement in April 2014 that said, among other things, "The GEM [Group of Eminent Persons] discussed thoroughly the need for entry into force of the CTBT in order to complete a global, legally-binding prohibition on nuclear weapon test explosions or other nuclear explosions. The Group also noted that entry into force and

---

[159] "Joint Ministerial Statement on the CTBT," New York, September 20, 2006, at http://www.armscontrol.org/pdf/20060920_CTBT_Joint_Ministerial_Statement.pdf#search=%22%20%22joint%20ministerial%20statement%20on%20the%20ctbt%22%22.

[160] George Shultz, William Perry, Henry Kissinger, and Sam Nunn, "A World Free of Nuclear Weapons," *Wall Street Journal*, January 4, 2007, p. 15.

[161] Mikhail Gorbachev, "The Nuclear Threat," *Wall Street Journal*, January 31, 2007, p. 13.

[162] Harold Brown and John Deutch, "The Nuclear Disarmament Fantasy," *Wall Street Journal*, November 19, 2007, p. 19.

[163] George Shultz, William Perry, Henry Kissinger, and Sam Nunn, "Toward a Nuclear-Free World," *Wall Street Journal*, January 16, 2008, p. 13.

[164] Testimony of Siegfried Hecker, former Director, Los Alamos National Laboratory, in U.S. Congress. Senate. Committee on Appropriations. Subcommittee on Energy and Water Development. Hearing on the Department of Energy and the U.S. Nuclear Weapon Non-Proliferation Efforts, 110th Congress, 2nd Session, April 30, 2008. Transcript by CQ Transcriptions.

[165] Australia. Department of Foreign Affairs and Trade. "Berlin Statement by Foreign Ministers on Nuclear Disarmament and Non-Proliferation," Berlin, April 30, 2011, http://www.dfat.gov.au/security/berlin_statement_110430 html. The statement is by foreign ministers of Australia, Canada, Chile, Germany, Japan, Mexico, the Netherlands, Poland, Turkey, and the United Arab Emirates.

[166] Preparatory Commission for the Comprehensive Nuclear-Test-Ban Treaty Organization, "Group of Eminent Persons (GEM)," http://www.ctbto.org/the-treaty/article-xiv-conferences/2013-conference-on-facilitating-the-entry-into-force-of-the-comprehensive-nuclear-test-ban-treaty-united-nations-new-york-usa/group-of-eminent-persons-gem/.

universalization of the CTBT would strengthen international disarmament efforts and the nuclear non-proliferation regime."[167]

The first Preparatory Committee meeting for the 2010 NPT Review Conference was held in Vienna, Austria, in April and May 2007. The chair of the committee released a paper that stated, "Strong support was expressed for the CTBT. The importance and urgency of its early entry into force was underscored. States which had not ratified the Treaty, especially those remaining 10 States whose ratification was necessary for its entry into force, were urged to do so without delay and without conditions."[168] A representative of Germany, speaking on behalf of the European Union, said, "The EU reiterates its call on States, particularly those listed in Annex II, to sign and ratify the said Treaty without delay and without conditions and, pending its entry into force to abide by a moratorium on nuclear testing and to refrain from any action contrary to the obligations and provisions of the CTBT."[169] The second Preparatory Committee meeting was held in Geneva in April and May 2008. At the meeting, several dozen states made statements in support of the CTBT and its entry into force.[170] The conference was held May 3-28, 2010; as noted earlier, many at the conference called for the CTBT to enter into force.

On September 24, 2008, the fourth CTBT Ministerial Meeting was held at U.N. headquarters; 96 nations signed a statement calling for signing and ratifying the treaty without delay and for continuation of the nuclear testing moratorium.[171] On December 2, 2008, the U.N. General Assembly adopted a resolution (document A/63/395) urging states to sign and ratify the CTBT; the vote was 175 in favor, 1 against (United States), and 3 abstentions (India, Mauritius, Syria).[172] In December 2008, the American Association for the Advancement of Science, the American Physical Society, and the Center for Strategic and International Studies issued a report, *Nuclear Weapons in 21st Century U.S. National Security*, that listed one component of "a possible new centrist package of nuclear initiatives" as a view commonly held by the committee, "Ratify the Comprehensive Nuclear-Test-Ban Treaty (CTBT), if coupled with other interconnected nuclear initiatives described below." These initiatives include, among many others, "development of an international nuclear forensics data bank," "pursuit of a Fissile Material Cut-Off Treaty," and "[t]he U.S. should continue to refurbish and update its stockpile as necessary without creating new nuclear weapon capabilities through the 'spectrum of options' approach."[173] The

---

[167] "Statement by the Group of Eminent Persons, Stockholm Meeting, 10-11 April 2014," http://www.ctbto.org/ fileadmin/user_upload/public_information/2014/Statement_of_GEM_Stockholm_FINAL.pdf.

[168] "2007 NPT PrepCom Chair's factual summary (now to be called a Chair's Paper)," May 11, 2007, available at http://www.acronym.org.uk/npt/chair.pdf.

[169] "First session of the Preparatory Committee for the 2010 Review Conference of the Parties to the Treaty on the Non-Proliferation of Nuclear Weapons, General Debate, Statement by Ambassador Rudiger Ludeking, Deputy Commissioner of the Federal Government [of Germany] for Arms Control and Disarmament on behalf of the European Union," Vienna, April 30, 2007 p. 5, available at http://www reachingcriticalwill.org/legal/npt/prepcom07/statements/ 30aprilEU.pdf.

[170] Reaching Critical Will, "Government Statements from the second session of the Preparatory Committee for the 2010 nuclear Non-Proliferation Treaty Review Conference

28 April 9–May 2008," at http://www.reachingcriticalwill.org/legal/npt/prepcom08/statements html.

[171] "Registration as UN Document of a Joint Statement of 4th Comprehensive Nuclear-Test-Ban Treaty (CTBT) Ministerial Meeting," States News Service, January 8, 2009.

[172] U.N. General Assembly. 63rd General Assembly. 61st Meeting (AM). "On Recommendation of First Committee, General Assembly Adopts 57 Texts ...," GA/10792, December 2, 2008.

[173] "Nuclear Weapons in 21st Century U.S. National Security," report by a joint working group of the American Association for the Advancement of Science, the American Physical Society, and the Center for Strategic and International Studies, December 2008, pp. ii, 7, 9.

Congressional Commission on the Strategic Posture of the United States released its report in May 2009 and was divided on the issue of U.S. ratification of the CTBT, the only issue on which it failed to reach agreement.[174] A Council on Foreign Relations task force, in a 2009 report, "believes that the benefits outweigh the costs and that the CTBT is in U.S. national security interests."[175] On September 23, 2010, 24 foreign ministers issued a joint statement on the CTBT calling on "all States that have not yet done so to sign and ratify the Treaty without delay" and committing themselves "to make the Treaty a focus of attention at the highest political level."[176] On December 2, 2011, the U.N. General Assembly adopted a resolution (A/RES/66/64) urging early entry into force of the CTBT; the vote was 175 in favor, 1 against (North Korea), and 3 abstentions (India, Mauritius, Syria). In contrast to the similar resolution in 2008, this resolution had the sponsorship of all five nuclear weapon states as recognized by the NPT.[177]

In September 2012, the Sixth Ministerial Meeting on the Comprehensive Nuclear-Test-Ban Treaty issued a statement reaffirming their "strongest support for the early entry into force" of the CTBT, called on states that have not done so to sign and ratify the treaty, noted that with the exception of North Korea, "the voluntary nuclear test moratorium has become a de facto international norm in the 21st Century," and pointed to advances made by the CTBTO Preparatory Commission in building the verification regime for the treaty.[178] On December 3, the U.N. General Assembly adopted a resolution urging states that have not done so to sign and ratify the CTBT. The vote was 184 for, 1 against (North Korea), and 3 abstentions (India, Mauritius, Syria).[179]

On December 5, 2013, the U.N. General Assembly adopted a resolution (A/RES/68/68) stressing the importance of early entry into force of the CTBT; the vote was 181 in favor, 1 against (North Korea), and 3 abstentions (India, Mauritius, Syria).[180] The Seventh Ministerial Meeting on the Comprehensive Nuclear-Test-Ban Treaty was held on

---

[174] Congressional Commission on the Strategic Posture of the United States. *America's Strategic Posture,* final report. Washington, DC, United States Institute of Peace Press, May 2009, pp. 81-87, http://www.usip.org/files/America's_Strategic_Posture_Auth_Ed.pdf.

[175] Council on Foreign Relations. Independent Task Force Report No. 62. *U.S. Nuclear Weapons Policy,* 2009, p. 89.

[176] "Joint Ministerial Statement on the CTBT," New York, September 23, 2010, http://www.ctbto.org/fileadmin/user_upload/public_information/2010/STATEMENTRev.16.09.pdf.

[177] United Nations. 66th General Assembly. "General Assembly Gravely Concerned about Status of UN Disarmament Machinery, Especially in Conference on Disarmament …," press release, December 2, 2011, document GA/11182, http://www.un.org/News/Press/docs//2011/ga11182.doc htm.

[178] For the final statement of the meeting, see "Joint Ministerial Statement on the CTBT," September 27, 2012, http://www.ctbto.org/fileadmin/user_upload/statements/CTBT_Joint_Ministerial_Statement_27_September_2012.pdf. Statements by participants in the meeting are available at http://www.ctbto.org/press-centre/highlights/2014/executive-secretary-meets-secretary-of-state-john-kerry-and-other-world-leaders/ (bottom of page).

[179] United Nations. General Assembly. "General Assembly, in Wake of High-Stakes Debate in First Committee that Championed Common Positions but Fell Short of Bridging Divides, Adopts 58 Texts," December 3, 2012, http://www.un.org/News/Press/docs//2012/ga11321.doc htm. The text of the resolution, number 67/76, "Comprehensive Nuclear-Test-Ban Treaty," is here: http://www.un.org/ga/search/view_doc.asp?symbol=A/RES/67/76.

[180] United Nations, 68th General Assembly, "Capping Intensive Disarmament Committee Session, General Assembly Adopts 53 Texts on Wide Range of Pressing International Security Concerns," press release, December 5, 2013, document GA/11463, http://www.un.org/News/Press/docs//2013/ga11463.doc htm. For text of the resolution, see United Nations, 68th General Assembly, Resolution adopted by the General Assembly on 5 December 2013 …

[A/Res]68/68. "Comprehensive Nuclear-Test-Ban Treaty," December 11, 2013, http://www.un.org/en/ga/search/view_doc.asp?symbol=A/RES/68/68.

September 26, 2014.[181] In addressing the meeting, Secretary of State John Kerry said, "So I come here to reiterate the Obama Administration's unshakable commitment to seeing this treaty ratified and entered into force. And though we have not yet succeeded in ratifying it for pure political, ideological reasons—not substance, I assure you—we nevertheless are pledged to live by it, and we do live by it, and we will live by it."[182]

See "CTBT Negotiations and the Nuclear Nonproliferation Treaty" for additional discussion of the relationship between the CTBT and NPT, including preparations for the 2015 NPT Review Conference.

Budget of the CTBTO Preparatory Commission

The PrepCom's assessed budget is presented in dollars *plus* euros. Its 2014 budget is $42.5 million plus €65.0 million, and as of September 2014 about 93 percent of this assessment had been collected.[183] (The PrepCom uses the calendar year as its fiscal year.) The U.S. assessment is 22.35% of the total.

U.S. funding for the PrepCom is FY2002 actual, $16.6 million; FY2003 actual, $18.2 million; FY2004 actual, $18.9 million; FY2005 actual, $18.8 million; FY2006 actual, $14.2 million; FY2007 actual, $13.5 million; and FY2008 appropriated, $23.8 million (net of an across-the-board cut in the Consolidated Appropriations Act). The FY2009 request was $9.9 million; P.L. 111-8, FY2009 Omnibus Appropriations Act, provided $25.0 million. The FY2010 appropriation was $30.0 million. FY2011 actual funding was $33.0 million plus a special contribution of $7.5 million. FY2012 actual funding was $33.0 million plus a special contribution of $8.9 million. FY2013 actual funding, reflecting the full-year continuing resolution, was $31.3 million plus a special contribution of $7.1 million. The FY2014 estimate was $31.0 million plus a special contribution of $1.0 million. The FY2015 request was $30.3 million plus a special contribution of $100,000. These funds are in the International Affairs budget under Nonproliferation, Antiterrorism, Demining, and Related Programs.[184] The Bush Administration's FY2007 budget justification stated that these funds "pay the U.S. share for the ongoing development and implementation of the International Monitoring System (IMS), which supplements U.S. capabilities to detect nuclear explosions. Since the United States does not seek ratification and entry-into-force of the CTBT, none of the funds will support Preparatory Commission activities that are not related to the IMS."[185] The Obama Administration has taken a different approach. In September 2009, Secretary of State Clinton said, "we are prepared to pay our share of the Preparatory Commission budget so that the global verification regime will be fully operational

---

[181] "Joint Ministerial Statement on the CTBT," September 26, 2014, New York, http://www.ctbto.org/fileadmin/ user_upload/statements/2014_minsterial_meeting/2014_joint_ministerial_statement_final.pdf.

[182] U.S. Department of State. "Remarks at the Friends of the Comprehensive Nuclear-Test-Ban Treaty Ministerial," John Kerry, Secretary of State, United Nations Headquarters, New York City, September 26, 2014, http://www.state.gov/secretary/remarks/2014/09/232219 htm.

[183] Comprehensive Nuclear-Test-Ban Treaty Preparatory Commission, "CTBTO Member States' Payment as at 19-Sep-2014," p. 4, http://www.ctbto.org/fileadmin/user_upload/treasury/38_19Sep2014_Member_States__Payments.pdf.

[184] For example, for the FY2015 request, see U.S. Department of State. *Congressional Budget Justification: Department of State, Foreign Operations, and Related Programs, Fiscal Year 2015,* March 2014, p. 168, http://www.state.gov/documents/organization/222898.pdf.

[185] U.S. Department of State. Summary and Highlights, *International Affairs Function 150, Fiscal Year 2007 Budget Request,* p. 40, at http://www.state.gov/documents/organization/60297.pdf.

when the CTBT enters into force."[186] In 2010, the United States paid off an outstanding prior years balance of $22.323 million.[187] The assessed contribution for the United States for 2012 was $11.6 million plus €13.4 million. As of December 21, 2012, the U.S. outstanding balance was $0.8 million plus €1.0 million, and the total outstanding balance for all member states was $12.8 million plus €4.0 million.[188]

The Administration's FY2011 request for the PrepCom was in two parts. A "voluntary contribution" of $33 million "helps to fund the establishment, operation, and maintenance of the worldwide International Monitoring System." In addition, "new for FY 2011, a voluntary contribution to the Preparatory Commission of the Comprehensive Nuclear-Test-Ban Treaty Organization ($10 million) will fund specific projects to increase the effectiveness and efficiency of the Treaty's verification regime."[189]

The Administration's FY2012 request for the PrepCom was in the same two parts, $33.0 million for the IMS and $7.5 million for specific projects.[190] In September 2011, Under Secretary Tauscher said that in August, the United States announced a contribution of $8.9 million to the CTBTO PrepCom "to support projects that will accelerate development of the CTBT verification regime," and in September, she said, the United States "concluded a Memorandum of Understanding with the Provisional Technical Secretariat to contribute up to $25.5 million to underwrite the rebuilding of the hydroacoustic monitoring station on Crozet Island in the southern Indian Ocean."[191]

The FY2013 request stated, "The voluntary contribution to the Preparatory Commission of the Comprehensive Nuclear-Test-Ban Treaty Organization ($33 million) helps to fund the establishment, operation, and maintenance of the worldwide International Monitoring System. In addition, $3.5 million will fund specific projects to increase the effectiveness and efficiency of the Treaty's verification regime."[192] For FY2014, the request is $31.0 million for the IMS and $1.0 million as special contributions. Among other things, the latter will assist the CTBTO's Provisional Technical Secretariat in "efforts to engage medical isotope producers to use techniques to reduce their xenon emissions, provide information on such emissions to the IDC, and begin defining how medical isotope data should be used when it is received by the IDC."[193] Since radioactive isotopes of xenon are a key signature of nuclear tests, reducing the emissions of these isotopes from sources other than nuclear tests and building a library of data on emissions

---

[186] Clinton, "Remarks at CTBT Article XIV Conference," p. 4.

[187] Comprehensive Nuclear-Test-Ban Treaty Preparatory Commission, "CTBTO Member States' Payment as at 05-Nov-2010," p. 4.

[188] Comprehensive Nuclear-Test-Ban Treaty Preparatory Commission, "CTBTO Member States' Payment as at 21-Dec-2012," p. 4, http://www.ctbto.org/fileadmin/user_upload/treasury/21Dec2012_Member_States_payments.pdf.

[189] U.S. Department of State. *Executive Budget Summary: Function 150 & Other International Programs Fiscal Year 2011*, 2010, pp. 81-82, http://www.state.gov/documents/organization/135888.pdf.

[190] U.S. Department of State. *Executive Budget Summary: Function 150 & Other International Programs, Fiscal Year 2012*, pp. 104-105, http://www.state.gov/documents/organization/156214.pdf.

[191] U.S. Department of State. Ellen Tauscher, Under Secretary for Arms Control and International Security, remarks at CTBT Article XIV Conference, New York, NY, September 23, 2011.

[192] U.S. Department of State. *Congressional Budget Justification*, Volume 2, Foreign Operations, Fiscal Year 2013, p. 126, http://www.state.gov/documents/organization/185014.pdf.

[193] U.S. Department of State, *Foreign Operations: Congressional Budget Justification, Fiscal Year 2014, Volume 2*, April 2013, p. 208, http://www.state.gov/documents/organization/208290.pdf.

from such sources should make it easier for the IDC to determine when a reading from IMS radionuclide detection stations is likely to indicate a nuclear test.

For 2014, the U.S. assessment was $9.5 million plus €14.6 million. At an exchange rate of €1 = $1.28, this assessment totaled approximately $28.2 million. As of September 13, 2014, the United States had paid its assessment in full.[194] As noted, the Administration's FY2015 request was $30.3 million plus a special contribution of $100,000.

Stockpile Stewardship

P5 states want to maintain their nuclear warheads under a CTBT and assert that they need computers and scientific facilities to do so. They also want to retain the ability to resume testing if other nations leave a CTBT, or if maintaining high confidence in key weapons requires testing. Nonnuclear nations fear that the P5 will continue to design new warheads under a CTBT, with computation and nonnuclear experiments replacing testing. Maintaining nuclear weapons, especially without testing, is termed "stockpile stewardship."

Congress established the National Nuclear Security Administration (NNSA) in Title XXXII of P.L. 106-65 (S. 1059), FY2000 National Defense Authorization Act, as a semiautonomous DOE agency to manage stewardship and related programs. In NNSA's budget, stewardship is funded by the Weapons Activities account, the main elements of which are Directed Stockpile Work, activities directly supporting weapons in the stockpile; Campaigns, technical efforts to develop and maintain capabilities to certify the stockpile for the long term; and Readiness in Technical Base and Facilities, mainly weapons complex infrastructure and operations. Weapons Activities contains other components as well. Weapons Activities appropriations were: FY2001, $5.006 billion; FY2002, $5.429 billion; FY2003, $5.954 billion; FY2004, $6.447 billion; FY2005, $6.626 billion; FY2006, $6.370 billion; FY2007, $6.259 billion; FY2008, $6.302 billion; FY2009, $6.380 billion; FY2010, $6.384 billion; FY2011, $6.896 billion; FY2012, $7.214 billion; and FY2013, $6.971 billion. The latter amount reflected the sequester and the across-the-board rescission.[195] The FY2014 enacted amount was $7.781 billion, and the FY2015 request was $8.315 billion.[196]

Stewardship is a contentious issue. It bears on Senate advice and consent to CTBT ratification. (It also was an issue in Senate debate on advice and consent to ratification of New START, the New Strategic Arms Reduction Treaty.) Beginning with the Nuclear Test Ban Treaty of 1963, the United States has implemented "safeguards," or unilateral steps to maintain nuclear security consistent with treaty limitations. President Kennedy's agreement to safeguards was critical for obtaining Senate approval of the 1963 treaty. Safeguards were modified in 1990 as part of the resolutions of ratification for the Threshold Test Ban Treaty and Peaceful Nuclear Explosions

---

[194] Comprehensive Nuclear-Test-Ban Treaty Preparatory Commission, "CTBTO Member States' Payments as at 19-Sep-2014," p. 4, http://www.ctbto.org/fileadmin/user_upload/treasury/38_19Sep2014_Member_States__Payments.pdf.

[195] The National Nuclear Security Administration provided CRS with information on the FY2013 appropriation, e-mail, June 4, 2013.

[196] U.S. Department of Energy. Office of Chief Financial Officer, *Department of Energy FY 2015 Congressional Budget Request*, Volume 1, National Nuclear Security Administration, DOE/CF-0096, Washington, DC, March 2014, p. 70, http://www.energy.gov/sites/prod/files/2014/03/f12/Volume_1_NNSA.pdf.

Treaty. The safeguards were modified again by President Clinton. In his August 11, 1995, speech announcing a zero-yield CTBT as a goal, he stated:

> As a central part of this decision, I am establishing concrete, specific safeguards that define the conditions under which the United States will enter into a comprehensive test ban. These safeguards will strengthen our commitments in the areas of intelligence, monitoring and verification, stockpile stewardship, maintenance of our nuclear laboratories, and test readiness.[197]

These safeguards are: Safeguard A: "conduct of a Science Based Stockpile Stewardship program to insure a high level of confidence in the safety and reliability of nuclear weapons in the active stockpile"; Safeguard B: "maintenance of modern nuclear laboratory facilities and programs"; Safeguard C: "maintenance of the basic capability to resume nuclear test activities prohibited by the CTBT"; Safeguard D: "a comprehensive research and development program to improve our treaty monitoring"; Safeguard E: intelligence programs for "information on worldwide nuclear arsenals, nuclear weapons development programs, and related nuclear programs"; and Safeguard F: the understanding that if the Secretaries of Defense and Energy inform the President "that a high level of confidence in the safety or reliability of a nuclear weapon type which the two Secretaries consider to be critical to our nuclear deterrent could no longer be certified, the President, in consultation with Congress, would be prepared to withdraw from the CTBT under the standard 'supreme national interests' clause in order to conduct whatever testing might be required."[198] The Clinton Administration transmitted the CTBT to the Senate with virtually identical safeguards in 1997, and the Senate modified these safeguards further in adopting an amendment to the resolution of ratification of the CTBT. (The amendment passed, but the resolution was defeated.)

Regarding the stewardship program, President Clinton said that the Secretary of Energy and the directors of the nuclear weapons laboratories had assured him that the United States could maintain its nuclear deterrent under a CTBT through a science-based stockpile stewardship program. "In order for this program to succeed," he said, "both the administration and the Congress must provide sustained bipartisan support for the stockpile stewardship program over the next decade and beyond."[199]

Safeguard F was codified by Section 3141 of P.L. 107-314, the FY2003 National Defense Authorization Act. As summarized by the State Department, this section provided that

> The Directors of the three DOE nuclear weapons laboratories—Los Alamos National Laboratory (LANL), Lawrence Livermore National Laboratory (LLNL), and Sandia National Laboratories (SNL)—are required to complete annual assessments of the safety, reliability, and performance of each weapon type in the nuclear weapons stockpile. In addition, the Commander of U.S. Strategic Command provides an assessment of the military effectiveness of the stockpile. These assessments also include a determination as to whether it is necessary

---

[197] President William J. Clinton, "Remarks Announcing a Comprehensive Nuclear Weapons Test Ban," August 11, 1995, in U.S. National Archives and Records Administration. Office of the Federal Register. *Weekly Compilation of Presidential Documents,* August 14, 1995, p. 1432.

[198] U.S. White House. Office of the Press Secretary. "Fact Sheet: Comprehensive Test Ban Treaty Safeguards," August 11, 1995, 1 p.

[199] President William J. Clinton, "Statement on a Comprehensive Nuclear Weapons Test Ban," August 11, 1995, in U.S. National Archives and Records Administration. Office of the Federal Register. *Weekly Compilation of Presidential Documents,* August 14, 1995, p. 1433.

to conduct an underground nuclear test to resolve any identified issues. The Secretaries of Energy and Defense are required to submit these reports unaltered to the President, along with any conclusions the Secretaries consider appropriate.[200]

As of September 2014, the laboratories had completed 18 annual assessments and the 19th was in progress.[201]

For a discussion of the possible role of updated safeguards in a future CTBT debate, see CRS Report R40612, *Comprehensive Nuclear-Test-Ban Treaty: Updated "Safeguards" and Net Assessments*, by Jonathan E. Medalia.

The ability of the stewardship program to maintain nuclear weapons without testing was a crucial issue in the 1999 Senate debate on the CTBT. The treaty's opponents claimed that stewardship offered no guarantee of maintaining weapons, and that experiments, computer models, and other techniques might offer no clue to some problems that develop over time. They further argued that it could be perhaps a decade before the tools for the program were fully in place, and by that time many weapon designers with test experience would have retired. Supporters held that the program was highly likely to work, with the stockpile already certified three times, and that safeguard "F" provided for U.S. withdrawal from the treaty in the event high confidence in a key weapon type could not be maintained without testing.

Several reports from 2009 raised concerns about stockpile stewardship. The Congressional Commission on the Strategic Posture of the United States observed, "The physical infrastructure is in serious need of transformation.... The intellectual infrastructure is also in serious trouble."[202] A Council on Foreign Relations task force found, "concerns about ensuring the highest caliber workforce at the weapons laboratories."[203] And a JASON report stated, "continued success of stockpile stewardship is threatened by lack of program stability, placing any LEP [life extension program] strategy at risk" and "the study team is concerned that this [nuclear weapons] expertise is threatened by lack of program stability, perceived lack of mission importance, and degradation of the work environment."[204] On the other hand, the latter report stated, "JASON finds no evidence that accumulation of changes incurred from aging and LEPs have increased risk to certification of today's deployed nuclear warheads," and "lifetimes of today's nuclear warheads could be extended for decades, with no anticipated loss in confidence, by using approaches similar to those employed in LEPs to date."[205] In January 2010, an op-ed by George Shulz, William Perry, Henry Kissinger, and Sam Nunn argued that "adequate and stable funding" for the nuclear weapons program was "urgently needed."[206]

---

[200] U.S. Department of State. Bureau of Arms Control, Verification, and Compliance. Fact Sheet: "Annual Assessment of the U.S. Nuclear Weapons Stockpile," December 18, 2012, http://www.state.gov/t/avc/rls/202013 htm.

[201] Information provided by Los Alamos National Laboratory, email, September 24, 2014.

[202] Congressional Commission on the Strategic Posture of the United States, *America's Strategic Posture,* p. 62.

[203] Council on Foreign Relations. Independent Task Force Report No. 62, *U.S. Nuclear Weapons Policy,* p. 76.

[204] "Lifetime Extension Program (LEP) Executive Summary," JASON Program Office, the MITRE Corporation, JSR-09334E, September 9, 2009, pp. 3-4, http://www.armscontrol.org/system/files/ JASON%20LEP%20REPORT%20SUMMARY%2009-09_0.pdf.

[205] Ibid., p. 2. Original text was bolded.

[206] George Shultz, William Perry, Henry Kissinger, and Sam Nunn, "How to Protect Our Nuclear Deterrent," *Wall Street Journal,* January 20, 2010, p. 17.

Section 1251 of the FY2010 National Defense Authorization Act (H.R. 2647, P.L. 111-84) required the President to submit a report on, among other things, a plan to enhance the safety, security, and reliability of the U.S. nuclear stockpile; modernize the nuclear weapons complex; and maintain nuclear weapon delivery platforms. On December 15, 2009, 40 Republican Senators and Senator Joseph Lieberman, in a letter to President Obama, cited Section 1251 and said that "a plan to modernize the U.S. nuclear deterrent" should include

> Full and timely Lifetime Extension Programs for the B61 and W76 warheads consistent with military needs.
>
> Funding for a modern warhead that includes new approaches to life extension involving replacement, or, possibly, component reuse.
>
> Full funding for stockpile surveillance work through the nuclear weapons complex, as well as the science and engineering campaigns at the national laboratories.
>
> Full funding for the timely replacement of the Los Alamos plutonium research and development and analytical chemistry facility, the uranium facilities at the Oak Ridge Y-12 plant, and a modern pit facility.[207]

The Administration took several actions in response to these concerns. Vice President Joe Biden wrote in January 2010, "For almost a decade, our [nuclear weapon] laboratories and facilities have been underfunded and undervalued." The FY2011 budget request for NNSA Weapons Activities, he continued, "reverses this decline and enables us to implement the president's nuclear-security agenda."[208] That budget, submitted in February, increased by $624.4 million, to $7,008.8 million. The Nuclear Posture Review, submitted in April, included a chapter, "Sustaining a Safe, Secure, and Effective Nuclear Arsenal," that called for extending the service life of nuclear warheads, increasing investment in the work force of the nuclear weapons complex, funding the Chemistry and Metallurgy Research Replacement Project at Los Alamos National Laboratory, and developing a new Uranium Processing Facility at the Y-12 National Security Complex.[209] In May, the President submitted New START to the Senate and provided a classified report as required by Section 1251 of the FY2010 National Defense Authorization Act. An unclassified one-page description of that report presented a cost projection for the nuclear weapons stockpile and infrastructure for FY2011-FY2020, and stated that "the Administration intends to invest $80 billion in the next decade to sustain and modernize the nuclear weapons complex."[210] The directors of the three nuclear weapons laboratories commented on the Nuclear Posture Review as follows:

> We believe that the approach outlined in the NPR, which excludes further nuclear testing and includes the consideration of the full range of life extension options (refurbishment of existing warheads, reuse of nuclear components from different warheads and replacement of nuclear components based on previously tested designs), provides the necessary technical flexibility to manage the nuclear stockpile into the future with an acceptable level of risk. We are reassured that a key component of the NPR is the recognition of the importance of supporting "a modern physical infrastructure–comprised of the national security laboratories

---

[207] The Honorable Mitch McConnell et al., letter to The Honorable Barack Obama, President, December 15, 2009.

[208] Vice President Joe Biden, "The President's Nuclear Vision," *Wall Street Journal*, January 29, 2010, p. 15.

[209] U.S. Department of Defense, *Nuclear Posture Review,* pp. 37-43.

[210] U.S. White House. "The New START Treaty—Maintaining a Strong Nuclear Deterrent," May 13, 2010, http://www.america.gov/st/texttrans-english/2010/May/20100514114003xjsnommis0.6300318.html.

and a complex of supporting facilities–and a highly capable workforce with the specialized skills needed to sustain the nuclear deterrent."[211]

Nonetheless, questions remained about the adequacy of stockpile stewardship, even as augmented, to sustain the nuclear arsenal. In letters to Representative Michael Turner, ranking Member, Subcommittee on Strategic Forces, Committee on Armed Services, Michael Anastasio, Director, Los Alamos National Laboratory, stated that "the available mitigation actions [for extending warhead lives], such as changes external to the nuclear package, or relaxation of certain military requirements, are reaching their limits." George Miller, Director, Lawrence Livermore National Laboratory, wrote, "The [warhead] surveillance program is becoming inadequate."[212] In a statement in April on the New START Treaty, Senators John McCain and Jon Kyl said, "We continue to believe it will be difficult for it to pass the Senate without the fully funded robust nuclear weapons modernization program required by section 1251 of the National Defense Authorization Act of 2010."[213] In a hearing on the nuclear weapons complex and New START in July, Senator Bob Corker said, "The issue that we're focused on today is the most crucial issue that we need to be focusing on … if you look at this 10-year plan [for Weapons Activities], that, in essence, we're still, even with the first year input that we have, which I think we all welcome, that there's still about a $10 billion shortfall to do the things that need to be done over this next 10 years to really modernize and do the things that we need to do."[214]

While the FY2011 Weapons Activities funding request provided a substantial increase over the FY2010 level, a key sticking point in the debate over New START was the level of funding the Administration would provide over the long term for the nuclear weapons program in general and the nuclear weapons complex in particular. According to a press article, "Republicans have sought some guarantee that promises in the Obama administration's 10-year plan to modernize the nuclear weapons complex will be carried out."[215] The Administration and Congress sought to meet these concerns. The FY2011 continuing resolution, P.L. 111-242 (H.R. 3081), maintained most spending at the FY2010 level, with few exceptions. One exception (Section 122) was to fund the Weapons Activities account at the rate requested for FY2011, $7,008.8 million, rather than at the FY2010 rate of $6,384.4 million. In November 2010, the Administration offered additional Weapons Activities funds. According to a press report, "Republicans have conditioned their support for the [New START] treaty on a big budget increase to fix up the country's aging weapons-production facilities." As a result, "in a last-minute bid to save [the treaty], the Obama administration has offered to spend $4 billion more over five years on the U.S. nuclear weapons complex."[216] The Administration presented this funding plan in a November 2010 update of the

---

[211] Sandia National Laboratories, "Tri-Lab Directors' Statement on the Nuclear Posture Review," press release, April 9, 2010, https://share.sandia.gov/news/resources/news_releases/tri-lab-directors%E2%80%99-statement-on-the-nuclear-posture-review/.

[212] U.S. Congress. House. Committee on Armed Services. "Turner Releases Lab Director Letters on JASON Life Extension Report in Advance of Nuclear Budget Hearing," press release, March 25, 2010, http://republicans.armedservices house.gov/news/PRArticle.aspx?NewsID=962. This document contains links to the letters from the three laboratory directors.

[213] "Statement by Senators Jon Kyl and John McCain on START Treaty," press release, April 8, 2010, http://kyl.senate.gov/record_print.cfm?id=323710.

[214] Statement by Senator Bob Corker, in U.S. Congress. Senate. Committee on Foreign Relations. Hearing on New START Treaty, July 15, 2010, transcript by CQ Transcriptions.

[215] Walter Pincus, "Similar Treaty but a Different Republican Reaction," *Washington Post*, August 10, 2010, p. 15.

[216] Mary Beth Sheridan and Walter Pincus, "Sources: $4 Billion Bid to Save START," *Washington Post*, November 13, 2010, p. 3.

1251 report. For FY2012, it called for an increase of $600 million, and for FY2012-FY2016 an increase of $4.1 billion, compared to the previously planned level.[217]

In response, Senators Kyl and Corker sent a memo on November 24 to Republican Members analyzing the revised funding plan. The memo stated, "In FY2010, the Obama administration invested only $6.4 billion in the National Nuclear Security Administration Weapons Activities funding line, a 20% loss in purchasing power from FY2005 alone." It further stated that only about $10 billion of the $80 billion in the original 1251 report was for new weapons activity. It found that the updated plan "satisfied many, but not all, of the initial questions we had earlier expressed." The memo noted several "remaining concerns," including a need for more funds for a uranium facility at Y-12 and a plutonium facility at Los Alamos, a commitment to advance funding for these facilities, and more funds (pending a review) for stockpile surveillance. Further, "The Administration should not engage in further cuts to our deployed or non-deployed stockpile without first determining if such cuts our in our national security interest and then obtaining corresponding reductions in other nations' nuclear weapons stockpiles, such as Russia's large stockpile of weapons not limited by New START (e.g., its tactical nuclear weapons)."[218]

In a letter of November 30 to the directors of Lawrence Livermore, Los Alamos, and Sandia National Laboratories, Senators Kerry and Lugar noted that the directors had testified in July that the original Section 1251 report was a good start but also expressed concerns. The Senators asked the directors for their opinion of the revised 1251 report.[219] In a letter of December 1, the directors responded that "we are very pleased by the update to the Section 1251 Report, as it would enable the laboratories to execute our requirements for ensuring a safe, secure, reliable and effective stockpile under the Stockpile Stewardship and Management Plan … it clearly responds to many of the concerns that we and others have voiced in the past about potential future-year funding shortfalls, and it substantially reduces risks to the overall program."[220]

As noted above, for FY2012, the House voted to authorize the amount requested for Weapons Activities, and the Senate Armed Services Committee recommended a reduction of $1 million. In contrast, the House voted to reduce Weapons Activities appropriations by $497.7 million from the request, and the Senate Appropriations Committee recommended a reduction of $439.7 million.

For FY2013, the Administration requested $7,577.3 million. This compares to a request of $7.9 billion projected in the November 2010 1251 report. Further, that report stated, "The Administration is committed to fully fund the construction of the Uranium Processing Facility

---

[217] U.S. "November 2010 Update to the National Defense Authorization Act of FY2010 Section 1251 Report: New START Treaty Framework and Nuclear Force Structure Plans," November 2010, p. 2, http://www.scribd.com/doc/43366094/Section-1251-Update-nov-2010. Hereinafter "November 2010 Update to the 1251 Report."

[218] "Memo from Sen. Jon Kyl, Sen. Bob Corker to Republican Members, November 24, 2010, re: Progress in Defining Nuclear Modernization Requirements," http://www.scribd.com/doc/44104068/Kyl-Corker-memo-to-Senate-colleagues-on-nuclear-modernization-11-24-2010.

[219] Letter to Michael Anastasio, Director, Los Alamos National Laboratory, from Senators Richard Lugar, Ranking Member, and John Kerry, Chairman, Senate Committee on Foreign Relations, November 30, 2010, http://lugar.senate.gov/issues/start/pdf/12012010Letters.pdf. (The Senators sent similar letters to the directors of Los Alamos and Sandia National Laboratories.)

[220] Letter to The Honorable John Kerry and The Honorable Richard Lugar, Senate Committee on Foreign Relations, from George Miller, Lawrence Livermore National Laboratory, Michael Anastasio, Los Alamos National Laboratory, and Paul Hommert, Sandia National Laboratories, December 1, 2010, 2 p., http://lugar.senate.gov/issues/start/pdf/12012010Letters2.pdf

(UPF) and the Chemistry and Metallurgy Research Replacement (CMRR)."[221] The CMRR Nuclear Facility (CMRR-NF), which was to have been completed in FY2023 on one spending path,[222] would have done analytical work on plutonium in support of pit production, permitting the existing pit production facility (PF-4, or Plutonium Facility 4, at Los Alamos) to manufacture 50 to 80 pits per year. However, the FY2013 request contained no funds for CMRR-NF, instead proposing "deferring CMRR Nuclear Facility construction for at least five years."[223] NNSA planned an alternative plutonium strategy, doing work that would have been done at CMRR-NF at other facilities, which would have permitted PF-4 to manufacture perhaps 20 to 30 pits per year. The request also proposed increasing spending on UPF above the figure projected in the 1251 report. The Administration had also stated in the 1251 report that the life extension program for the W76 warhead "will be fully funded for the life of the program at $255 million annually,"[224] but requested $174.9 million.

The change to CMRR-NF was particularly controversial. Thomas D'Agostino, Under Secretary for Nuclear Security and Administrator, National Nuclear Security Administration, presented the case for deferring the facility to the Senate Appropriations Committee:

> in close consultation with our national laboratories and national security sites, we are adjusting our plutonium strategy by deferring for at least five years construction of the Chemistry and Metallurgy Research Replacement Nuclear Facility (CMRR-NF) project at Los Alamos National Laboratory and focusing instead on how we can meet our plutonium needs on an interim basis by using the capabilities and expertise found at existing facilities. Utilizing existing facilities will allow us to meet anticipated near term requirements for plutonium operations while focusing on other key modernization projects. Deferring CMRR-NF will have an estimated cost avoidance from 2013 to 2017 that totals approximately $1.8 billion, which will help offset the costs of other priorities such as Weapons Lifetime Extension programs and other infrastructure needs.[225]

The appropriations committees provided no funds for the facility, as requested. The Armed Services Committees took a different view. The FY2013 defense authorization bill (H.R. 4310) as passed by the House expressed the sense of Congress that up to $160 million in prior year funds should be used to continue design and construction of CMRR-NF in FY2013. The Senate Armed Services Committee report on FY2013 defense authorizations stated,

> The committee is strongly concerned with the budget proposal to defer "by at least 5 years" the replacement project for the Chemistry and Metallurgy Research Replacement Nuclear Facility (CMRR-NF) building at Los Alamos National Laboratory, New Mexico.

---

[221] "November 2010 Update to the 1251 Report," p. 5.

[222] Ibid., p. 6.

[223] U.S. Department of Energy. *FY 2013 Congressional Budget Request: Volume 1, National Nuclear Security Administration*, pp. 185.

[224] "November 2010 Update to the 1251 Report," p. 4.

[225] "Statement of Thomas P. D'Agostino, Undersecretary for Nuclear Security and Administrator, National Nuclear Security Administration, U.S. Department of Energy, on the Fiscal Year 2013 President's Budget Request Before the Senate Appropriations Committee Subcommittee on Energy and Water Development, March 21, 2012," pp. 5-6, available via http://www.appropriations.senate.gov/ht-energy.cfm?method=hearings.view&id=efa574fe-712c-40f4-a8b2-c5a782bbd5f0.

A deferral "for at least 5 years" appears to be a cancellation. Based on the analysis the committee has received to date, it appears that such a cancellation would have an adverse impact on nuclear modernization programs.[226]

The committee recommended authorizing $150.0 million for CMRR-NF construction out of funds appropriated for Weapons Activities for FY2013. In response, a Statement of Administration Policy on the Senate bill stated,

> The Administration strongly objects to section 3111, which would require construction of the Chemistry and Metallurgy Research Replacement (CMRR) facility to begin in 2013. The Departments of Defense and Energy agree that, in light of today's fiscal environment, CMRR can be deferred for at least five years, and funds reallocated to support higher priority nuclear weapons goals. An interim strategy will be implemented to provide adequate support to plutonium pit manufacturing and storage needs until a long-term solution can be implemented.[227]

Section 3114 of the conference report (H.Rept. 112-705), as passed by both houses, required among other things that

- CMRR-NF be built;

- its cost may not exceed $3.7 billion (unless the Secretary of Energy submits a detailed justification to Congress for any increase);

- the building must commence operations by December 31, 2026;

- $70.0 million in FY2013 NNSA funds be available for construction of CMRR-NF;

- prior year funds authorized for the CMRR project be available for construction of CMRR-NF; and

- any alternative plutonium strategy must include full operational capability of CMRR-NF by December 31, 2026.

However, the conference report authorized no construction funds for this project for FY2013, and as of late December 2012, a Los Alamos Site Office spokeswoman reportedly said that "all planned closure elements" for CMRR-NF were "essentially completed."[228]

The Administration's departure from the budget plan presented in the November 2010 1251 report may have ramifications for any future Senate consideration of the CTBT. A letter to Secretary of Defense Leon Panetta from Senator Jon Kyl and seven other Senators urged continuation of CMRR-NF with operation by 2024. It stated, "We believe that the linkage between nuclear modernization and the New START Treaty was clearly defined at the time of

---

[226] U.S. Congress, Senate Committee on Armed Services, *National Defense Authorization Act for Fiscal Year 2013*, Report to accompany S. 3254, 112th Cong., 2nd sess., June 4, 2012, S.Rept. 112-173 (Washington: GPO, 2012), pp. 287-288.

[227] U.S. White House. Executive Office of the President. Office of Management and Budget. "Statement of Administration Policy: S. 2354—National Defense Authorization Act for FY 2013," November 29, 2012, http://www.whitehouse.gov/sites/default/files/omb/legislative/sap/112/saps3254s_20121129.pdf.

[228] Todd Jacobson, "In Final Defense Authorization Act, Congress Looks to Revive CMRR-NF," *Nuclear Weapons & Materials Monitor,* December 21, 2012, p. 4.

ratification and remains so today. Thus, we are concerned about the impact that failing to fulfill this critical commitment could have on future treaties the Senate may be asked to consider."[229]

The FY2015 budget request included out-year figures for Weapons Activities. For the years FY2015-FY2019, the table below compares figures from the FY2015 request with those from the November 2010 update to the 1251 report.

Table 1. Projected Budgets for Weapons Activities, FY2015-FY2019 ($ billions)

Using figures from the FY2015 NNSA budget request and the November 2010 update to the 1251 report

	FY2015	**FY2016**	**FY2017**	**FY2018**	**FY2019**
FY2015 NNSA request	8.315	8.907	9.261	9.477	9.702
Nov. 2010 1251 report	8.7	8.9	8.9-9.0	9.2-9.3	9.4-9.6

Sources: U.S. Department of Energy. Office of Chief Financial Officer. FY 2015 Congressional Budget Request, Volume 1, National Nuclear Security Administration, DOE/CF-0096, March 2014, pp. 70, 75; and U.S. White House. November 2010 Update to the National Defense Authorization Act of FY2010 Section 1251 Report: New START Treaty Framework and Nuclear Force Structure Plans, p. 9, http://www.lasg.org/CMRR/Sect1251_update_17Nov2010.pdf.

For FY2015, the Administration is developing a plutonium strategy that includes updating pit production equipment in PF-4; moving some operations out of PF-4 to make more space for pit production; cleaning out the vault in PF-4 that stores nuclear materials and moving excess plutonium to the Waste Isolation Pilot Plant; using the Radiation Laboratory/Utility/Office Building (RLUOB), a building completed in FY2010 near PF-4, for work supporting pit production; building "modules" (buried concrete structures to be located near PF-4) to provide added space for plutonium work; and reusing retired pits in warhead life extension programs. NNSA anticipates that these and related activities will provide the capacity to manufacture 30 pits per year by 2026; other steps are being considered to boost pit production up to 80 pits per year by 2030.[230] NNSA provides details on its plans in its *Stockpile Stewardship and Management Plan*.[231] Two CRS reports deal with pit production.⌐

Subcritical experiments (SCEs): As part of the stockpile stewardship program, NNSA is conducting SCEs. It states, "Subcritical experiments examine the behavior of plutonium as it is strongly shocked by forces produced by chemical high explosives.... The experiments are subcritical; that is, no critical mass is formed and no self-sustaining nuclear chain reaction can occur; thus, there is no nuclear explosion."[232] SCEs are conducted at Nevada National Security

---

[229] Letter from Senators Jon Kyl, Ben Nelson, John McCain, Joe Lieberman, Bob Corker, Johnny Isakson, James M. Inhofe, and Kelly Ayotte to The Honorable Leon E. Panetta, Secretary of Defense, June 29, 2012, http://freebeacon.com/wp-content/uploads/2012/07/Kyl-et-al-nuclear.pdf.

[230] Presentation by Lt. Gen. Frank Klotz (USAF, Ret.), Administrator, National Nuclear Security Administration, presentation at conference, "The Strategic Nuclear Enterprise: Implementing the Roadmap Ahead," September 18, 2014, Washington, DC.

[231] U.S. Department of Energy, *Fiscal Year 2015 Stockpile Stewardship and Management Plan*, Report to Congress, Washington, DC, April 2014, http://nnsa.energy.gov/sites/default/files/nnsa/04-14-inlinefiles/2014-04-11%20FY15SSMP_FINAL_4-10-2014.pdf.

[232] U.S. Department of Energy. National Nuclear Security Administration. Nevada Site Office. "NNSA Conducts Pollux Subcritical Experiment at Nevada National Security Site, news release, December 6, 2012, (continued...)

Site (NNSS, formerly Nevada Test Site, NTS). All SCEs but one have been conducted in the U1a tunnel complex, about 1,000 feet underground at NNSS. That complex could contain explosions up to 500 pounds of explosive and associated plutonium. Another SCE, "Unicorn," was conducted in a "down-hole" or vertical shaft configuration similar to an underground nuclear test, not in a tunnel, to exercise operational readiness.[233] SCEs try to determine if radioactive decay of aged plutonium would degrade weapon performance. Several SCEs have been used to support certification of the W88 pit. (A pit is the "trigger" of a thermonuclear weapon.) In 1998, Secretary of Energy Bill Richardson called SCEs "a key part of our scientific program to provide new tools and data that assess age-related complications and maintain the reliability and safety of the nation's nuclear deterrent."[234] As they produce no chain reaction, the Clinton Administration saw them as consistent with the CTBT. Critics counter that they would help design new weapons without testing; are unnecessary; may look like nuclear tests if not monitored intrusively; and are inconsistent with the spirit of a CTBT, which, critics believe, is aimed at halting nuclear weapons development, not just testing. NNSA stated that subcritical experiments cost between $5 million and $30 million.[235] (For further information on subcritical experiments and test readiness, see CRS Report RL32130, *Nuclear Weapon Initiatives: Low-Yield R&D, Advanced Concepts, Earth Penetrators, Test Readiness*, by Jonathan E. Medalia.)

As of September 2014, there have been 27 SCEs: *1997:* Rebound, July 2; Holog, September 18; *1998:* Stagecoach, March 25; Bagpipe, September 26; Cimarron, December 11; *1999:* Clarinet, February 9; Oboe, September 30; Oboe 2, November 9; *2000:* Oboe 3, February 3; Thoroughbred, March 22; Oboe 4, April 6; Oboe 5, August 18; Oboe 6, December 14; *2001:* Oboe 8, September 26; Oboe 7 (held after Oboe 8), December 13; *2002:* Vito (jointly with UK), February 14; Oboe 9, June 7; Mario, August 29; Rocco, September 26; *2003:* Piano, September 19; *2004:* Armando, May 25; *2006:* Krakatau (jointly with UK), February 23; Unicorn, August 30; *2010:* Bacchus, September 15; Barolo A, December 1; *2011:* Barolo B, February 2; *2012:* Pollux, December 5. An NNSA official stated that, for Pollux, "Diagnostic equipment fielded by our scientists resulted in more data collected in this single experiment than all other previous subcritical experiments." Another official said, "Pollux will provide a significant data set to verify [computer] codes important to laboratories' stockpile missions."[236] There may be an SCE in FY2015.[237]

Other experiments: The laboratories have conducted two other types of experiments involving plutonium at NNSS. "Thermos" experiments are material property studies. NNSA stated in March 2007 that they do not use enough plutonium to sustain a chain reaction, and the plutonium "does not approximate any part of weapons design." Twelve such experiments were conducted between

---

(...continued)

http://nnsa.energy.gov/mediaroom/pressreleases/pollux120612.

[233] "Nanos Tours Nevada Test Site," *Daily Newsbulletin,* Los Alamos National Laboratory, November 10, 2003, at http://www.lanl.gov/orgs/pa/newsbulletin/2003/11/10/text04.shtml.

[234] U.S. Department of Energy. "DOE to Conduct Fourth Subcritical Experiment; Scientific Data to Help Ensure the Safety and Reliability Of the Stockpile Without Nuclear Testing," press release, September 23, 1998.

[235] U.S. Department of Energy. Office of Management, Budget and Evaluation/CFO. *FY 2006 Congressional Budget Request.* Volume 1, National Nuclear Security Administration. DOE/ME-0046, February 2005, p. 88, at http://www.mbe.doe.gov/budget/06budget/Content/Programs/Vol_1_NNSA_2.pdf.

[236] U.S. Department of Energy. National Nuclear Security Administration. "NNSA Conducts Pollux Subcritical Experiment at Nevada National Security Site," press release, December 6, 2012, http://nnsa.energy.gov/mediaroom/ pressreleases/pollux120612.

[237] Information provided by National Nuclear Security Administration, email, September 25, 2014.

February and May 2007; none had been conducted since then as of August 2011.[238] The Joint Actinide Shock Physics Experimental Research (JASPER) Facility is a gas gun that shoots a high-velocity projectile at a plutonium target to produce "high shock pressures, temperatures, and strain rates similar to that of a nuclear weapon" in the plutonium. According to NNSA, the resulting data help "refine the computer codes used to certify the U.S. nuclear stockpile."[239] As of August 2011, 88 JASPER experiments had been conducted between March 2001 and April 2011, of which 34 used plutonium and 54 used surrogate materials. From the third quarter of FY2011 through FY2012, NNSA conducted 13 JASPER experiments, of which 7 used plutonium.[240] For FY2013, there were 13 experiments at JASPER, 7 of which used plutonium.[241] Another five JASPER experiments, one of which used plutonium, were conducted through June 2014, the most recent data available.[242]

In addition to JASPER, NNSA facilities conduct other types of experiments in support of stockpile stewardship, including the following, described in an NNSA report of June 2014: the Dual-Axis Radiographic Hydrodynamic Test (DARHT) Facility at Los Alamos, which provides radiographic images of "moving, non-nuclear weapon assemblies"; the Contained Firing Facility, operated by Livermore at a remote site, which also provides radiographic images of "moving, non-nuclear weapon assemblies" but "has a substantially larger field of view than DARHT"; the National Ignition Facility at Livermore, which is used to investigate properties of materials, radiation, plasma, and other aspects of nuclear explosions at temperatures and pressures "not possible on any other experimental platform"; the Z-Machine at Sandia, for investigating properties of material, plasma, and radiation; Omega, a laser facility at the University of Rochester for studying properties of material, plasma, and radiation at high temperatures and pressures; the High Explosive Application Facility at Livermore, which studies properties of chemical explosives; high explosive facilities at Los Alamos, which use various types of equipment "to investigate fundamental properties and reactions of chemical explosives, detonators, and to conduct studies on materials; the Los Alamos Neutron Science Center (LANSCE), which generates neutrons to study material properties; proton radiography at Los Alamos, which uses LANSCE "to produce protons for radiography of static and dynamic materials"; the Big Explosives Experimental Facility at NNSS, which studies "materials as they are merged together by high-explosives detonations"; TA-55 at Los Alamos, which has facilities to investigate properties of plutonium and other metals; and the U1a facility at NNSS for conducting subcritical experiments.[243] "Hydrodynamic experiments" are also conducted at NNSS.

---

[238] Information provided by National Nuclear Security Administration, Nevada Site Office, personal communication, August 3, 2011.

[239] U.S. Department of Energy. National Nuclear Security Administration. Nevada Site Office. "Joint Actinide Shock Physics Experimental Research (JASPER)," DOE/NV-1015, September 2004, at http://www nv.doe.gov/library/factsheets/DOENV_1015.pdf.

[240] U.S. Department of Energy. National Nuclear Security Administration. "Summary of Experiments Conducted in Support of Stockpile Stewardship," October 2012 (covers FY2012 by quarter), http://nnsa.energy.gov/sites/default/files/nnsa/12-12-inlinefiles/2012-12-06%20Quarterly%20SSP%20Experiment%20Summary-FY12-4Q.pdf, and November 2011 (covers FY2011 by quarter), http://nnsa.energy.gov/sites/default/files/nnsa/inlinefiles/Quarterly%20SSP%20Experiment%20Summary-FY11-4Q%20FINAL.pdf.

[241] U.S. Department of Energy. National Nuclear Security Administration. "Summary of Experiments Conducted in Support of Stockpile Stewardship," October 2013, p. 3, http://nnsa.energy.gov/sites/default/files/nnsa/2013-10-29%20Quarterly%20SSP%20Experiment%20Summary-FY13-4Q%20final.pdf.

[242] U.S. Department of Energy. National Nuclear Security Administration. "Summary of Experiments Conducted in Support of Stockpile Stewardship," June 2014, p. 3, http://nnsa.energy.gov/sites/default/files/nnsa/06-14-inlinefiles/2014-06-04%20Quarterly%20SSP%20Experiment%20Summary-Q2FY14_complete_rjh%20final.pdf.

[243] Ibid., entire document (4 p.).

These "involve non-nuclear surrogate materials that mimic many of the properties of nuclear materials. Hydrodynamics refers to the physics involved when solids, under extreme conditions, begin to mix and flow like liquids." One experiment, "Leda," conducted August 12, 2014, "consisted of a plutonium surrogate material and high explosives to implode a 'weapon-relevant geometry.'"[244] According to NNSA, Leda "was a preparatory experiment for the next series of subcritical experiments."[245]

Test Readiness: President Clinton directed DOE to be prepared to conduct a nuclear test within three years of a decision to do so. Yet a September 2002 report by DOE's Office of Inspector General found this ability "at risk."[246] In January 2002 the Nuclear Posture Review briefing called for an unspecified acceleration of nuclear test readiness, and in March 2002 the Panel to Assess the Reliability, Safety, and Security of the United States Nuclear Stockpile assessed that "test readiness should be no more than three months to a year."[247] The FY2003 National Defense Authorization Act, P.L. 107-314, Section 3142, required the Secretary of Energy to report on alternative test readiness postures and recommend the optimal readiness posture. The resulting report argued that the three-year posture was increasingly at risk and recommended moving to an 18-month readiness posture by the end of FY2005.[248]

The FY2004 Weapons Activities request included $24.9 million to reduce the posture from three years to 18 months. The National Defense Authorization Act and the Energy and Water Development Appropriations Act provided the funds requested. Conferees on the latter expected NNSA to focus on a program that can meet the current 24-month requirement "before requesting significant additional funds to pursue a more aggressive goal of an 18-month readiness posture."[249] In contrast, the FY2004 National Defense Authorization Act (P.L. 108-136, §3112) stated, "Commencing not later than October 1, 2006, the Secretary of Energy shall achieve, and thereafter maintain, a readiness posture of not more than 18 months for resumption by the United States of underground tests of nuclear weapons."

In testimony before the Senate Armed Services Committee on March 24, 2004, NNSA Administrator Linton Brooks said that NNSA's goal "is to achieve the 18-month test readiness posture called for in the Defense Authorization Act."[250] The FY2005 National Defense Authorization Act provided the full $30.0 million requested for test readiness. In the FY2005

---

[244] Los Alamos National Laboratory, "Los Alamos Conducts Important Hydrodynamic Experiment in Nevada," September 8, 2014, http://www.lanl.gov/discover/news-release-archive/2014/September/09.08-nevada-hydrodynamic-experiment.php.

[245] Information provided by National Nuclear Security Administration, email, September 25, 2014.

[246] U.S. Department of Energy. Office of Inspector General. Office of Audit Services. *National Nuclear Security Administration's Test Readiness Program*, Audit Report, September 2002, p. 1.

[247] Letter report from John Foster, Chairman, Panel to Assess the Reliability, Safety, and Security of the United States Nuclear Stockpile, to Senator Carl Levin, Chairman, Committee on Armed Services, U.S. Senate, March 15, 2002, p. ES-2, at http://www.fas.org/nuke/control/ctbt/text/foster01.doc.

[248] U.S. Department of Energy. National Nuclear Security Administration. *Nuclear Test Readiness.* Report to Congress, April 2003, p. 5-8.

[249] U.S. Congress. Committee of Conference. *Making Appropriations for Energy and Water Development for the Fiscal Year Ending September 30, 2004, and for Other Purposes,* H.Rept. 108-357, to accompany H.R. 2754, 108th Congress, 1st Session, 2003, p. 159-160.

[250] U.S. Congress. Senate. Committee on Armed Services. Subcommittee on Strategic Forces. Hearing on strategic forces, March 24, 2004, transcript by FDCH e-Media, Inc. Testimony of Ambassador Linton Brooks, Administrator, National Nuclear Security Administration.

energy and water bill, the House Appropriations Committee recommended reducing the Primary Assessment Technologies campaign request of $81.5 million, which included $30.0 million for test readiness, by $15.0 million "to limit the enhanced test readiness initiative to the goal of achieving a 24-month test readiness posture. The Committee continues to oppose the 18-month test readiness posture."[251] The FY2005 Consolidated Appropriations Act reduced this campaign by $7.5 million.

NNSA's FY2006 test readiness request was $25.0 million "to continue improving the state of readiness to reach an 18-month test-readiness posture in FY2006."[252] In a Senate Armed Services Committee hearing on February 15, 2005, Senator John Warner asked Secretary of Energy Samuel Bodman whether DOE would meet the 18-month test readiness requirement by October 1, 2006. Secretary Bodman replied, "We continue to be committed to that requirement of the law" and was informed that DOE is on track to meet the October 1 deadline.[253] In testimony before the Senate Appropriations Committee's Energy and Water Development Subcommittee on April 14, 2005, Ambassador Brooks explained the rationale for the 18-month posture: "Shorter than that, and you were paying money for readiness you couldn't use, because the experiment [the nuclear test] wouldn't be ready. Longer than that, and you were running the risk of being ready to test to find out whether you had corrected an important problem, but the test site wasn't ready."[254] The House Appropriations Committee continued to favor a 24-month posture and stated that the Reliable Replacement Warhead program "obviates any reason to move to a provocative 18-month test readiness posture."[255] The Energy and Water Development Appropriations Act reduced test readiness funding to $20.0 million; conferees directed DOE to maintain the 24-month posture. The National Defense Authorization Act also provided $20.0 million; the accompanying conference report did not address the readiness posture.

For FY2007, NNSA requested $14.8 million for test readiness and noted that the target test readiness posture for FY2006-FY2011, 24 months, was achieved in FY2005.[256] The House Armed Services Committee's report on FY2007 defense authorization stated, "While the committee has no indication of the need to resume underground nuclear testing in the near future, it does believe that maintaining the 18 month readiness posture as directed by Congress is important to national security. The committee notes that funding shortfalls have precluded the Department of Energy from achieving the 18 month readiness posture as required by law."[257] In the FY2007 Energy and Water Development Appropriations Bill (H.R. 5427), the House provided the requested amount, and the Senate Appropriations Committee (in S.Rept. 109-274)

---

[251] U.S. Congress. House. Committee on Appropriations. *Energy and Water Development Appropriations Bill, 2005,* H.Rept. 108-554, to accompany H.R. 4614, 108th Congress, 2nd Session, 2004, p. 116.

[252] Department of Energy, *FY 2006 Congressional Budget Request,* Volume 1, p. 93.

[253] U.S. Congress. Senate. Committee on Armed Services. Hearing on FY2006 budget request for Atomic Energy Defense Activities of DOE and NNSA, February 15, 2005, transcript by FDCH e-Media, Inc. Testimony of Samuel Bodman, Secretary of Energy.

[254] U.S. Congress. Senate. Committee on Appropriations. Subcommittee on Energy and Water Development. Hearing on FY2006 appropriations for NNSA, April 14, 2005, transcript by FDCH e-Media, Inc. Testimony of Ambassador Linton Brooks, Under-secretary, Nuclear Security, [and] Administrator, National Nuclear Security Administration.

[255] U.S. Congress. House. Committee on Appropriations. *Energy and Water Development Appropriations Bill, 2006.* H.Rept. 109-86, to accompany H.R. 2419, 109th Congress, 1st Session, 2005, p. 134.

[256] Department of Energy, *FY 2007 Congressional Budget Request.* Volume 1, National Nuclear Security Administration, p. 97.

[257] U.S. Congress. House. Committee on Armed Services. *National Defense Authorization Act for Fiscal Year 2007,* H.Rept. 109-452 to accompany H.R. 5122, 109th Congress, 2nd Session, 2006, p. 464.

recommended providing that amount. NNSA requests no funds under test readiness for FY2008, noting that the program has achieved its goal of a 24-month readiness posture, current capabilities will be maintained through other parts of the budget, and "a more forward looking program is planned."[258] The House Armed Services Committee made no mention of test readiness in its report, while the Senate Armed Services Committee provided no funds, as requested. The House Appropriations Committee sharply criticized the decision not to request funds, and added funds:

> The Committee supports the 24-month test readiness posture at the Nevada Test Site and provides an additional $20,000,000 to restore the funding in the Administration's budget request which terminated the activity. The Committee is baffled by the Administration's decision to eliminate funding for nuclear test readiness after four budget cycles of insisting that shortening to an 18-month test readiness posture was required for national security reasons.... In the fiscal year 2008 budget request, the NNSA proposes what the Committee believes to be a wasteful investment by allowing the restored test readiness activities to be degraded.[259]

Section 3112 of the conference version of H.R. 1585, the FY2008 defense authorization bill, repealed a provision (P.L. 108-136, §3113; 50 U.S.C. 2528a) requiring an 18-month nuclear test posture, and required the Secretary of Energy to submit a report on nuclear test readiness every two years. For test readiness, the FY2008 estimate is $4.9 million and the FY2009 request is $10.4 million.[260] NNSA stated that it had achieved a 24-month test readiness posture in FY2007, but that "forecasted budget levels resulted in a change in the test readiness posture target to 24 to 36 months."[261] The FY2009 defense authorization bills as passed by the House and as reported by the Senate Armed Services Committee include the requested amount for test readiness. The House Appropriations Committee recommended eliminating FY2009 funds for test readiness. It stated that the "outstanding Stockpile Stewardship program ... has performed better than expected and has created a technically superior alternative to nuclear testing," and "the Committee finds no evidence that nuclear testing would add a useful increment to the immense and expanding body of weapons knowledge arising from Stockpile Stewardship."[262] The joint explanatory statement (submitted in lieu of a conference report) on S. 3001, Duncan Hunter National Defense Authorization Act for FY2009, provided $5.4 million for test readiness.[263] According to NNSA, "The responsibility for the maintenance of infrastructure and physical assets at the NTS transferred to the RTBF program in FY 2010."[264]

---

[258] U.S. Department of Energy. Office of Chief Financial Officer. *FY 2008 Congressional Budget Request.* Volume 1, National Nuclear Security Administration. DOE/CF-014, February 2007, p. 101. Available at http://www.mbe.doe.gov/budget/08budget/Content/Volumes/Vol_1_NNSA.pdf.

[259] U.S. Congress. House. Committee on Appropriations. *Energy and Water Development Appropriations Bill, 2008,* H.Rept. 110-185, to accompany H.R. 2641, 110th Congress, 1st Session, 2007, p. 102.

[260] Department of Energy, *FY2009 Congressional Budget Request,* vol. 1, p. 133.

[261] Ibid., p. 135.

[262] U.S. Congress. House. Committee on Appropriations. *Energy and Water Development Appropriations Bill, 2009,* unnumbered committee print, 110th Congress, 2nd Session, June 2008, p. 126.

[263] U.S. Congress. House. Committee on Armed Services. *Duncan Hunter National Defense Authorization Act for Fiscal Year 2009,* joint explanatory statement to accompany S. 3001, Committee Print HASC No. 10, 110th Congress, 2nd Session, 2008, p. 799.

[264] Department of Energy, *FY 2011 Congressional Budget Request,* vol. 1, p. 94. RTBF, Readiness in Technical Base and Facilities, is a major component of the Weapons Activities budget. It funds the operation and maintenance of weapons complex facilities and the planning and construction of facilities and infrastructure.

Regarding test readiness, NNSA stated in November 2010, "There is no separate funding designated for Test Readiness in FY2011 nor was there in FY2010. Test Readiness is supported through the work accomplished in the Stockpile Stewardship Program and specifically by the experiments that are conducted at the Nevada National Security Site in U1a that exercise the expertise necessary to resume underground testing if necessary." NNSA stated in regard to test readiness posture, "The required posture is to be able to conduct a test in the time frame required by Presidential Decision Directive 15. Current test readiness is 24 to 36 months. The range is intentionally vague as it covers a spectrum of possible test scenarios. The specific tests scenarios are classified."[265] A DOE report of May 2011 provides further details.[266]

Table 2. U.S. Nuclear Tests by Calendar Year

1945-1949	6	1960-1964	202	1980-1984	92
1950-1954	43	1965-1969	231	1985-1989	75
1955-1959	145	1970-1974	137	1990-1992	23
		1975-1979	100	Total	1054

Source: U.S. Department of Energy.

Notes: These figures include all U.S. nuclear tests, of which 24 were joint U.S.-UK tests conducted at the Nevada Test Site between 1962 and 1991. They reflect data on unannounced tests that DOE declassified on December 7, 1993. They exclude the two atomic bombs that the United States dropped on Japan in 1945. On June 27, 1994, Secretary O'Leary announced that DOE had redefined three nuclear detonations (one each in 1968, 1970, and 1972) as separate nuclear tests. This table reflects these figures. She also declassified the fact that 63 tests, conducted from 1963 through 1992, involved more than one nuclear explosive device.

CTBT Pros and Cons

The CTBT is contentious. For a detailed analysis of the case for and against the treaty, see CRS Report RL34394, *Comprehensive Nuclear-Test-Ban Treaty: Issues and Arguments*, by Jonathan E. Medalia. Key arguments include the following:

Can the United States maintain deterrence without testing? The treaty's supporters hold that the U.S. stockpile stewardship program can maintain existing, tested weapons without further testing. Indeed, as of September 2014, the weapons laboratories had completed 18 annual assessments of the stockpile, with the 19th in progress.[267] Treaty supporters claim that these weapons meet any deterrent needs, so that new types are not needed. Opponents maintain that there can be no confidence in existing warheads because many minor modifications over time will change them from tested versions. As a result, some opponents argue that testing is needed to restore and maintain confidence, while others believe that testing may become needed and the option to return to testing must not be ruled out. Opponents see deterrence as dynamic, requiring new types of nuclear weapons to counter new threats, and assert that these weapons must be tested.

Are monitoring and verification capability sufficient? "Monitoring" refers to technical capability; "verification" to its adequacy to maintain security. Supporters hold that advances in monitoring,

---

[265] Information provided to CRS via email by the National Nuclear Security Administration, November 29, 2010.

[266] U.S. Department of Energy. "Nuclear Test Readiness." Report to Congress, May 2011.

[267] Information provided by Los Alamos National Laboratory, email, September 24, 2014.

such as the rollout of the International Monitoring System, make it hard for an evader to conduct undetected tests. They claim that any such tests would be too small to affect the strategic balance. Opponents see many opportunities for evasion, such as detonating an explosion in a large underground cavity to muffle its seismic waves. They believe that clandestine tests of even small weapons could put the United States at a serious disadvantage.

How might the treaty affect nuclear nonproliferation and disarmament? Supporters claim that the treaty makes technical contributions to nonproliferation, such as limiting weapons programs; some supporters believe that nonproliferation requires progress toward nuclear disarmament, with the treaty a key step. They note that all NATO members excepting the United States have ratified the CTBT. Opponents believe that a strong nuclear deterrent is essential for nonproliferation because it reduces the incentive for friends and foes alike to build their own nuclear weapons, that nonproliferation and disarmament are unrelated, and that the international community gives this nation little credit for its many nonproliferation and disarmament actions.

The National Academy of Sciences Study and Its Critics

In 2012, debate over the CTBT continued as a major study was released and was met by some criticism. On March 30, 2012, a committee of the National Academy of Sciences (NAS) released its report, *The Comprehensive Nuclear Test Ban Treaty: Technical Issues for the United States.*[268] The report was intended to update a similar NAS report issued in 2002[269] to reflect more recent developments. It found considerable improvement in U.S. ability to maintain nuclear weapons without nuclear-explosive testing as a result of progress in the stockpile stewardship program, and considerable improvement in U.S. and international ability to detect clandestine nuclear tests as a result of the rollout of the International Monitoring System and improved technical capabilities. It stated that further progress is likely in the ability to detect nuclear tests, and that continued and improved ability to maintain the U.S. nuclear stockpile depends on sustained support. It also stated that some actions could occur even under a CTBT, such as development of simple nuclear weapons by states that do not currently possess them, and that not every threat would require a return to U.S. nuclear testing. Key findings of the report include the following:

- "The technical capabilities for maintaining the U.S. stockpile absent nuclear-explosion testing are better now than anticipated by the *2002 Report.*" (p. 4)

- "Provided that sufficient resources and a national commitment to stockpile stewardship are in place, the committee judges that the United States has the technical capabilities to maintain a safe, secure, and reliable stockpile of nuclear weapons into the foreseeable future without nuclear-explosion testing." (p. 4)

- "One of the major advances in monitoring in the last 10 years is that most of the IMS seismic stations are operating now.... The threshold levels for IMS seismic detection are now well below 1 kt worldwide for fully coupled explosions." (p. 6)

---

[268] National Academy of Sciences. National Research Council. Committee on Reviewing and Updating Technical Issues Related to the Comprehensive Nuclear Test Ban Treaty. *The Comprehensive Nuclear Test Ban Treaty— Technical Issues for the United States.* Washington, National Academies Press, 2012.

[269] National Academy of Sciences. Committee on Technical Issues Related to Ratification of the Comprehensive Nuclear Test Ban Treaty. *Technical Issues Related to the Comprehensive Nuclear Test Ban Treaty.* Washington, National Academy Press, 2002.

- In the past 10 years, the IMS radionuclide network has gone from being essentially non-existent to a nearly fully functional and robust network with new technology that has surpassed most expectations." (p. 7)

- A strong national commitment to recruiting and sustaining a high-quality workforce; recapitalizing aging infrastructure and force structure; and strengthening the science, engineering, and technology base is essential to sustaining a safe, secure, and reliable stockpile, as well as necessary explosion-monitoring capability for the United States." (p. 8)

- "There is currently no mechanism that would enable Congress to assess whether the U.S. CTBT safeguards were being fulfilled after entry into force." (p. 9)

- Russia and China are unlikely to be able to deploy new types of strategic nuclear weapons that fall outside of the design range of their nuclear-explosion test experience without several multi-kiloton tests to build confidence in their performance. Such multi-kiloton tests would likely be detectable (even with evasion measures) by appropriately resourced U.S. national technical means and a completed IMS network." (p. 11)

- "Other States intent on acquiring and deploying modern, two-stage thermonuclear weapons would not be able to have confidence in their performance without multi-kiloton testing. Such tests would likely be detectable (even with evasion measures) by appropriately resourced U.S. national technical means and a completed IMS network." (p. 11)

While there has not been a report of similar detail rebutting the 2012 NAS report, there have been several criticisms. C. Paul Robinson, former Director of Sandia National Laboratories, pointed to a finding in the report (p. 10) that certain evasion methods "are credible only for device yields below a few kilotons worldwide and at most a few hundred tons at well-monitored locations." Robinson stated that tests at such yield could be of significant value.[270] Jack Murphy, a seismologist with SAIC, commented on seismic monitoring aspects of the NAS report.[271] Among his comments:

- "all of the quantitative monitoring analyses presented in the report simply assume that detection equals identification.... in general the two thresholds are significantly different." (p. 1)

- The NAS report states, "A CTBTO on-site inspection (OSI) would have a high likelihood of detecting evidence of a nuclear explosion with yield greater than about 0.1 kilotons, provided that the event could be located with sufficient precision in advance and that the OSI was conducted without hindrance." Murphy responds, "While a specific quantitative value (0.1 kt) is cited for the yield threshold, the significance of this finding remains unclear. What is the definition of 'a high likelihood of detecting evidence'? What is the definition of

---

[270] Presentation at Heritage Foundation, "Comprehensive Test Ban Treaty: Questions and Challenges," symposium, April 10, 2012, http://www.heritage.org/events/2012/04/ctbt.

[271] J.R. Murphy, "Comments on the Seismic Monitoring Analyses Presented in the 2012 National Academy of Sciences Report: 'The Comprehensive Nuclear Test Ban Treaty—Technical Issues for the United States," unpublished paper, 2012.

'sufficient precision' in the location estimate? If it is say better than 5 km, where would such a precise location estimate come from?" (p. 2)

- The NAS report has a table marked "for the 10% detection probability which the Committee judges is the largest that would be used by a potential evader for planning purposes." Murphy comments, "Once again this equates detection to identification and monitoring capability. Why 10%? The discussion ignores the uncertainty associated with the fact that, while the 90% detection thresholds are generally fairly well constrained by observations, the 10% detection thresholds are not and basically correspond to extrapolations based on an assumed statistical distribution model." (p. 3)

In addition, some have pointed to the many caveats, qualifications, and imprecise wordings in the report as indicating considerable uncertainty. For example:

"*Provided that sufficient resources and a national commitment to stockpile stewardship are in place,* the committee judges that the United States has the technical capabilities to maintain a safe, secure, and reliable stockpile of nuclear weapons into the foreseeable future without nuclear-explosion testing. Sustaining these technical capabilities will require at least … A Strong Scientific and Engineering Base … A Vigorous Surveillance Program … Modernized Production Facilities … A Competent and Capable Workforce," among other things. (p. 4, italics added) Critics would note that Congress did not provide the full amount requested for Weapons Activities for FY2012, and that the Administration requested less for FY2013 than it had indicated in the November 2010 1251 report, calling into question the sufficiency both of resources and of a national commitment to stockpile stewardship.

"The threshold levels for IMS seismic detection are now well below 1 kt worldwide *for fully coupled explosions.*" (p. 6, italics added) Critics would note that a fully coupled explosion is perhaps the least likely form of test that a determined evader would use because full coupling (i.e., with no space between the explosive device and the soil or rock) would readily transmit seismic signals. Instead, in this view, evaders might use decoupling (detonating a device in a large cavity so as to muffle the seismic signal), detonating a device in a remote ocean area so that it would not be attributable to the tester even though it would be detected, or other evasion scenarios.

"A CTBTO on-site inspection (OSI) would have a high likelihood of detecting evidence of a nuclear explosion with yield greater than about 0.1 kilotons, *provided that the event could be located with sufficient precision in advance and that the OSI was conducted without hindrance.*" (p. 8, italics added) In addition to the comments from Murphy, above, critics would note that it is highly probable that a nation that had conducted a clandestine nuclear test would hinder an OSI in every way possible, such as by refusing entry for the OSI team, delays, noncooperation, lack of support, or sabotage. Such tactics would imply that the nation had something to hide, but could prevent inspectors from finding evidence of a test.

Chronology

09/26/14—The seventh CTBT Ministerial Meeting was held at U.N. Headquarters in New York.

09/04/14—The Republic of the Congo ratified the CTBT.

08/18/14—The CTBTO Preparatory Commission inaugurated a new facility to train personnel and to test equipment for infrasound (low-frequency sound) and seismic detection of nuclear explosions.

08/11/14—A report indicated that activity at North Korea's nuclear test site "has come to a standstill," judging from satellite imagery.

06/16-17/14—The CTBTO Preparatory Commission held its 42nd meeting; the next is scheduled for October 28-30.

06/4-5/14—The G7 summit in Brussels adopted a declaration on nonproliferation and disarmament calling, among other things, for early entry into force and universalization of the CTBT.

03/04/14—Niue became the 162nd state to ratify the CTBT.

06/17/13—The Comprehensive Nuclear-Test-Ban Treaty Organization Preparatory Commission (CTBTO PrepCom) Science and Technology Conference is scheduled for June 17-21.

06/13/13—The CTBTO PrepCom's 40th session is scheduled for June 13-14. This will be the last PrepCom of Executive Secretary Tibor Tóth, whose term ends on July 31. His successor, Lassina Zerbo, takes office the next day.

06/10/13—Fifty years ago, President Kennedy delivered his American University Commencement Address, in which he proposed a comprehensive test ban treaty and declared a moratorium on U.S. atmospheric nuclear testing.

06/06/13—The House Armed Services Committee passed H.R. 1960, the FY2014 defense authorization bill, 59-2. It included an amendment that passed by voice vote fencing certain funds until the President certifies that no state party to the CTBT has conducted certain nuclear weapon tests, and barring use of U.S. contributions to the CTBTO PrepCom for lobbying or advocacy in the United States relating to the CTBT.

04/22/13—The second session of the Preparatory Committee for the 2015 Nuclear Non-Proliferation Treaty Review Conference was held April 22-May 3. Delegates called for entry into force of the CTBT and referenced the final document of the 2010 review conference, which stressed the urgency of entry into force.

04/08/13—Between April 8 and 14, International Monitoring System stations detected radioactive isotopes of xenon consistent with the North Korean nuclear test of February 12.

2/12/13—North Korea conducted a nuclear test.

2/08/13—Chad ratified the CTBT.

12/07/12—By a vote of 184 for, 1 against (North Korea), and 3 abstentions, the U.N. General Assembly adopted a resolution urging countries that have not done so to sign and ratify the CTBT.

12/05/12—Staff from Los Alamos and Sandia National Laboratories and the Nevada National Security Site (NNSS) conducted the 27th subcritical experiment, "Pollux," at NNSS.

10/23/12—Lassina Zerbo was elected to be the next Executive Secretary of the CTBT Organization Preparatory Commission.

10/22/12—The Comprehensive Nuclear-Test-Ban Treaty Organization Preparatory Commission began its 39th meeting, which ended October 24.

09/27/12—A group of foreign ministers issued a statement reaffirming their strongest support for the CTBT.

04/09/12—Niue became the 183rd state to sign the CTBT.

03/30/12—The National Research Council of the National Academy of Sciences released the unclassified version of its report, *The Comprehensive Nuclear Test Ban Treaty—Technical Issues for the United States.*

02/06/12—Indonesia became the 157th state to ratify the CTBT, and the 36th of the 44 Annex 2 states whose ratification is required for entry into force.

12/02/11—The U.N. General Assembly adopted Resolution A/RES/66/64, "Comprehensive Nuclear-Test-Ban Treaty," on a vote of 175 for, 1 against (North Korea), and 3 abstentions (India, Mauritius, Syria). The resolution, among other things, "Stresses the vital importance and urgency of signature and ratification, without delay and without conditions, in order to achieve the earliest entry into force of the Comprehensive Nuclear-Test-Ban Treaty."

10/24/11—The Preparatory Commission for the Comprehensive Nuclear-Test-Ban Treaty Organization endorsed a budget of $10.3 million for an integrated field exercise in 2014. This exercise is intended to improve the organization's on-site inspection capabilities.

09/23/11—A conference on accelerating CTBT entry into force was held at U.N. headquarters in New York.

09/20/11—Guinea became the 155th state to ratify the CTBT.

08/29/11—The second International Day Against Nuclear Tests was observed.

06/14/11—Ghana ratified the CTBT.

06/00/11—The Preparatory Commission for the Comprehensive Nuclear-Test-Ban Treaty sponsored a conference, "Comprehensive Nuclear-Test-Ban Treaty: Science and Technology 2011," in Vienna, Austria, from June 8 to 10.

05/10/11—Ellen Tauscher, Under Secretary of State for Arms Control and International Security, said, "The Obama Administration is preparing to engage the Senate and the public on an education campaign that we expect will lead to ratification of the CTBT."

04/30/11—Foreign ministers from 10 nations issued a statement in support of the CTBT.

03/00/11—The National Institute for Public Policy released a report suggesting that "U.S. ratification of the CTBT would bring few if any tangible benefits while introducing significant new risks for U.S. and allied security."

11/00/10—The Comprehensive Nuclear-Test-Ban Treaty Organization Preparatory Commission held a simulated on-site inspection in Jordan from November 1 to 12.

10/05/10—Assistant Secretary of State Rose Gottemoeller said, "The Administration prepares for U.S. Senate reconsideration of the Treaty."

09/23/10—Twenty-four foreign ministers issued a joint statement on the CTBT calling on "all States that have not yet done so to sign and ratify the Treaty without delay" and committing themselves "to make the Treaty a focus of attention at the highest political level."

09/15/10—NNSA conducted the 24th subcritical experiment, "Bacchus," at the Nevada Nuclear Security Site. This was the first such experiment in four years.

08/29/10—U.N. General Assembly resolution 64/35, adopted by consensus on December 3, 2009, declared this day the International Day Against Nuclear Tests.

05/26/10—Central African Republic and Trinidad and Tobago ratified the CTBT.

05/03/10—At the 2010 NPT Review Conference, Indonesia announced that it "is initiating the process of the ratification of the Comprehensive Nuclear-Test-Ban Treaty." Indonesia is one of the 44 nations that must ratify the treaty for it to enter into force.

05/00/10—The eighth Nuclear Nonproliferation Treaty Review Conference was held May 3-28 at U.N. headquarters in New York. The final document stated, "The Conference reaffirms the vital importance of the entry into force of the Comprehensive Nuclear-Test-Ban Treaty as a core element of the international nuclear disarmament and non-proliferation regime."

For earlier chronology, see the **Appendix**.

For Additional Reading

2010 Review Conference of the Parties to the Treaty on the Non-Proliferation of Nuclear Weapons, "Final Document," New York, 2010, http://www.un.org/ga/search/view_doc.asp?symbol=NPT/CONF.2010/50%20(VOL.I).

American Association for the Advancement of Science, American Physical Society, and Center for Strategic and International Studies, Joint Working Group, "Nuclear Weapons in 21st Century U.S. National Security," December 2008.

"*Arms Control Today* 2008 Presidential Q&A: President-elect Barack Obama," *Arms Control Today,* December 2008, pp. 31-36.

Arms Control Association, *CTBT at 15: Status and Prospects,* report on a conference held February 17, 2012, at Vienna Center for Disarmament and Non-Proliferation, Vienna, Austria, October 2012, http://www.armscontrol.org/files/ACA_CTBT_Report_Vienna_2012.pdf.

Australia. Department of Foreign Affairs and Trade. "Berlin Statement by Foreign Ministers on Nuclear Disarmament and Non-proliferation," April 30, 2011, http://www.dfat.gov.au/security/berlin_statement_110430.html.

Bailey, Kathleen, and Robert Barker. "Why the United States Should Unsign the Comprehensive Test Ban Treaty and Resume Nuclear Testing." *Comparative Strategy.* April-June 2003: 131-138.

Bailey, Kathleen, and Thomas Scheber, *The Comprehensive Test Ban Treaty: An Assessment of the Benefits, Costs, and Risks,* National Institute for Public Policy, March 2011, xix + 65 p., http://www.nipp.org/CTBT%203.11.11%20electronic%20version.pdf.

Brown, Harold, and John Deutch. "The Nuclear Disarmament Fantasy." *Wall Street Journal,* November 19, 2007, p. 19.

Brumfiel, Geoff, "Isotopes Hint at North Korean Nuclear Test," *Nature,* February 3, 2012, http://www.nature.com/news/isotopes-hint-at-north-korean-nuclear-test-1.9972. [Addresses De Geer's article on North Korea]

Center for Security Policy, "Towards a New Deterrent: Analysis and Recommendations for the Commission on the Strategic Posture of the United States," 5 p., c. May 2008, http://www.centerforsecuritypolicy.org/modules/newsmanager/ center%20publication%20pdfs/towards%20a%20new%20deterrent%20516.pdf.

Collina, Tom, with Daryl Kimball, *Now More Than Ever: The Case for the Comprehensive Nuclear Test Ban Treaty,* Arms Control Association, February 2010.

Conference on Facilitating the Entry into Force of the Comprehensive Nuclear-Test-Ban Treaty, "Final Declaration and Measures to Promote the Entry into Force of the Comprehensive Nuclear-Test-Ban Treaty," September 27, 2013, 5 p. + app., http://www.ctbto.org/fileadmin/ user_upload/Art_14_2013/Statements/Final_Declaration.pdf.

Congressional Commission on the Strategic Posture of the United States. *America's Strategic Posture,* final report. Washington, DC, United States Institute of Peace Press, May 2009.

Corden, Pierce, and David Hafemeister, "Nuclear Proliferation and Testing: A Tale of Two Treaties," *Physics Today,* April 2014, pp. 41-46.

Council on Foreign Relations. Independent Task Force Report No. 62. *U.S. Nuclear Weapons Policy,* 2009.

Dahlman, Ola, Jenifer Mackby, Svein Mykkeltveit, and Hein Haak, *Detect and Deter: Can Countries Verify the Nuclear Test Ban?,* Dordrecht, Netherlands, Springer, 2011, 271 p.

De Geer, Lars-Erik, "Radionuclide Evidence for Low-Yield Nuclear Testing in North Korea in April/May 2010," *Science and Global Security,* 20 (2012), pp. 1-29, http://www.tandfonline.com/doi/pdf/10.1080/08929882.2012.652558.

Dodge, Michaela, and Baker Spring, "Keeping Nuclear Testing on the Table: A National Security Imperative," Heritage Foundation Backgrounder no. 2770, February 28, 2013, http://report.heritage.org/bg2770.

Feith, Douglas, Frank Gaffney, James Lyons, and R. James Woolsey, "Obama's Harmful Nuclear Illusions," *Washington Post,* March 31, 2013, p. 15.

Gallucci, Robert, "Nuclear Shockwaves: Ramifications of the North Korean Nuclear Test," *Arms Control Today,* November 2006.

Gorbachev, Mikhail, "The Nuclear Threat," *Wall Street Journal,* January 31, 2007, p. 13.

Gottemoeller, Rose, remarks at the American Bar Association Spring Meeting, International Law Section, Washington, DC, April 25, 2013, http://translations.state.gov/st/english/texttrans/2013/04/20130429146553.html#axzz2VLXX3DnP

Graham, Owen, "Consider Tech Risk When Debating Nuclear Test Ban Treaty," *Defense News* (online), June 17, 2012, http://www.defensenews.com/article/20120617/DEFFEAT05/306170007/Consider-Tech-Risk-When-Debating-Nuclear-Test-Ban-Treaty?odyssey=nav|head.

Grossman, Elaine, "U.S. General Wants to Retain Nuclear Test Option," *Global Security Newswire,* July 22, 2008.

Hafemeister, David, "The Comprehensive Test Ban Treaty: Effectively Verifiable," *Arms Control Today,* October 2008.

Hafemeister, David, "Progress in CTBT Monitoring Since Its 1999 Senate Defeat," *Science and Global Security,* no. 15, 2007, pp. 151-183.

Harden, Blaine, "North Korean Nuclear Blast Draws Global Condemnation," *Washington Post,* May 26, 2009, p. 1.

Heller, Arnie, "Enhancing Confidence in the Nation's Nuclear Stockpile," *Science & Technology Review,* July/August 2010, pp. 4-11.

Hoffman, David, "Supercomputers Offer Tools for Nuclear Testing—and Solving Nuclear Mysteries," *Washington Post,* November 1, 2011, p. 1.

Horovitz, Liviu, "A Detour Strategy for the Test Ban Treaty," *Washington Quarterly,* Fall 2011, pp. 87-99.

"Joint Ministerial Statement on the CTBT," New York, September 23, 2010, 3 p., http://www.ctbto.org/fileadmin/user_upload/public_information/2010/STATEMENTRev.16.09.pdf.

Jonas, David, and Thomas Saunders, "The Object and Purpose of a Treaty: Three Interpretive Methods," *Vanderbilt Journal of Transnational Law,* vol. 43, no. 3, May 2010, pp. 565-609.

Joseph, Jofi, "Renew the Drive for CTBT Ratification" *Washington Quarterly,* April 2009, pp. 79-90, http://www.twq.com/09april/docs/09apr_Joseph.pdf.

Kazakhstan, Embassy of, et al., "Nuclear Weapons Testing: History, Progress, Challenges," conference held September 15, 2014, Washington, DC; transcript at http://www.armscontrol.org/events/Nuclear-Weapons-Testing_History-Progress-Challenges.

Kerry, John, "New Directions for Foreign Relations," *Boston Globe,* January 13, 2009.

Kimball, Daryl, "Learning from the 1999 Vote on the Nuclear Test Ban Treaty," *Arms Control Today,* October 2009, pp. 46-52.

Kimball, Daryl, "Time to Move Forward on the Test Ban Treaty," *Arms Control Today,* April 2013, http://www.armscontrol.org/act/2013_04/Focus.

Klug, Foster, and Matthew Pennington, "Photos Show NKorea Nuclear Readiness," Associated Press/ABC News, December 28, 2012, http://abcnews.go.com/International/wireStory/ap-exclusive-photos-show-nkorea-nuclear-readiness-18079671.

Kyl, Senator Jon, "Why We Need to Test Nuclear Weapons," *Wall Street Journal,* October 21, 2009, p. 23.

Kyl, Senator Jon, and Richard Perle, "Our Decaying Nuclear Deterrent," *Wall Street Journal,* June 29, 2009, p. 13.

Lakshmi, Rama, "Key Indian Figures Call for New Nuclear Tests Despite Deal with U.S.," *Washington Post,* October 5, 2009, p. 7.

Linzer, Dafna, and Thomas Ricks, "U.S. Waits for Firm Information on Nature and Success of [North Korean Nuclear] Device," *Washington Post,* October 11, 2006: 14.

Mathews, Jessica Tuchman, "This Time, Ban the Test," *International Herald Tribune,* October 21, 2009.

Monroe, Robert, "A Critical Moment in History," remarks at Exchange Monitor's First Annual Nuclear Deterrence Summit, December 4, 2008, 3 p.

Monroe, Robert, "Assessing Risks of Comprehensive Test Ban Treaty," June 15, 2012, video, http://www.youtube.com/watch?v=h9plbibJ74Y&list=UUPPw4A4ZmhK_e95S2Ka0Xaw&index=2&feature=plcp.

Monroe, Robert, "The Antiquation of America's Nuclear Weapons," *Washington Times,* March 4, 2013.

Murphy, Jack, "Comments on the Seismic Monitoring Analyses Presented in the 2012 National Academy of Sciences Report: 'The Comprehensive Nuclear Test Ban Treaty – Technical Issues for the United States,'" spring 2012 (technical criticisms of the report by an SAIC seismologist)

National Academy of Sciences. "Advances in Nuclear-Test Monitoring and Verification," briefing slides by five presenters, September 24, 2012, available via http://cstsp.aaas.org/content.html?contentid=2507.

National Academy of Sciences. Committee on Technical Issues Related to Ratification of the Comprehensive Nuclear Test Ban Treaty. *Technical Issues Related to the Comprehensive Nuclear Test Ban Treaty.* Washington, National Academies Press, 2002. http://www.nap.edu/catalog.php?record_id=10471.

National Academy of Sciences, National Research Council, Committee on Reviewing and Updating Technical Issues Related to the Comprehensive Nuclear Test Ban Treaty, *The*

Comprehensive Nuclear Test Ban Treaty—Technical Issues for the United States, Washington, National Academies Press, 2012, http://www.nap.edu/catalog.php?record_id=12849. [updates 2002 report]

O'Leary, Hazel, "New Evidence for the Nuclear Test-Ban Treaty," *San Diego Union-Tribune,* April 19, 2012, http://www.utsandiego.com/news/2012/apr/19/new-evidence-for-the-nuclear-test-ban-treaty/.

Pabian, Frank, and Siegfried Hecker, "Contemplating a Third Nuclear Test in North Korea," *Bulletin of the Atomic Scientists* (online edition), August 6, 2012.

Preparatory Committee for the 2015 Review Conference of the Parties to the Treaty on the Non-Proliferation of Nuclear Weapons, Second Session (April 22-May 3, 2013), "Comprehensive Nuclear-Test-Ban Treaty," Working paper submitted by the members of the Non-Proliferation and Disarmament Initiative (Australia, Canada, Chile, Germany, Japan, Mexico, the Netherlands, Poland, Turkey and the United Arab Emirates), March 6, 2013, NPT/CONF.2015.PC.II/WP-1, http://papersmart.unmeetings.org/media/1104226/NPTCONF.2015PC.IIWP.1.pdf

Preparatory Commission for the Comprehensive Nuclear-Test-Ban Treaty Organization, website, http://www.ctbto.org.

Preparatory Commission for the Comprehensive Nuclear-Test-Ban Treaty Organization, *Annual Report 2013,* June 2014, c. 90 p., http://www.ctbto.org/fileadmin/user_upload/pdf/Annual_Report_2013/English/AR2013-English-Opening.pdf.

Preparatory Commission for the Comprehensive Nuclear-Test-Ban Treaty, "CTBTO detects radioactivity consistent with 12 February announced North Korean nuclear test," press release, April 23, 2013, http://www.ctbto.org/press-centre/press-releases/2013/ctbto-detects-radioactivity-consistent-with-12-february-announced-north-korean-nuclear-test/.

Preparatory Commission for the Comprehensive Nuclear-Test-Ban Treaty, IFE14 [Integrated Field Exercise 2014] home page, http://www.ctbto.org/specials/integrated-field-exercise-2014/.

Preparatory Commission for the Comprehensive Nuclear-Test-Ban Treaty, *CTBTO Spectrum* (journal), August 2014, http://www.ctbto.org/publications/spectrum-publication/spectrum-issues-2012-and-onward/issue-22-august-2014/.

"Project for the Comprehensive Nuclear Test Ban Treaty," website sponsored by the Arms Control Association, http://projectforthectbt.org/.

Ramaker, Jaap, Jenifer Mackby, Peter Marshall, and Robert Geil, *The Final Test: A History of the Comprehensive Nuclear-Test-Ban Treaty Negotiations,* Vienna, Austria, Provisional Technical Secretariat of the Preparatory Commission for the Comprehensive Nuclear-Test-Ban Treaty Organization, 2003, 291 p.

Richards, Paul, "Forensic Seismology and CTBT Verification," *CTBTO Spectrum,* January 2007, pp. 1, 6, 19.

Russian Federation. Ministry for Atomic Energy and Ministry of Defense. *USSR Nuclear Weapons Tests and Peaceful Nuclear Explosions, 1949 through 1990.* 1996. 63 p.

Russian Federation. Ministry for Atomic Energy. *Catalog of Worldwide Nuclear Testing.* 1999. http://www.iss.niiit.ru/ksenia/catal_nt/.

Sanger, David, "North Koreans Say They Tested Nuclear Device," *New York Times,* October 9, 2006, p. 1.

Sanger, David, and Choe Sang-Hun, "North Korea Confirms It Conducted 3d Nuclear Test," *New York Times* (online edition), February 12, 2013.

Schneidmiller, Chris, "As Obama Prepares to Push Nuclear Test Ban, Technological Basis Still Debated," *Global Security Newswire,* July 15, 2011, and "Senate Decision Key to Future of Test Ban Treaty," *Global Security Newswire,* July 18, 2011 (two-part series).

Shultz, George, William Perry, Henry Kissinger, and Sam Nunn, "A World Free of Nuclear Weapons," *Wall Street Journal,* January 4, 2007, p. 15.

Shultz, George, William Perry, Henry Kissinger, and Sam Nunn, "Toward a Nuclear-Free World," *Wall Street Journal,* January 16, 2008, p. 13.

Shultz, George, William Perry, Henry Kissinger, and Sam Nunn, "How to Protect Our Nuclear Deterrent," *Wall Street Journal,* January 20, 2010, p. 17.

Spring, Baker, *Restoring the Role of the Nation-State System in Arms Control and Disarmament,* Heritage Foundation Special Report SR-84, September 21, 2010, http://thf_media.s3.amazonaws.com/2010/pdf/SR84.pdf.

Sokolski, Henry, and Gary Schmitt, "Advice for the Nuclear Abolitionists," *Weekly Standard,* May 12, 2008.

UK Prime Minister's Office. "UK-France Summit 2010 Declaration on Defence and Security Co-operation," November 2, 2010.

Umarov, Ambassador Kairat, Daryl Kimball, and Paul Walker, "Close the Door on Nuclear Dangers," The Hill, September 14, 2014, http://thehill.com/blogs/congress-blog/foreign-policy/217596-close-the-door-on-nuclear-dangers.

U.N.. "Resolution adopted by the General Assembly on 5 December 2013 [on the report of the First Committee (A/68/417)], 68/68. Comprehensive Nuclear-Test-Ban Treaty," A/Res/68/68, December 11, 2013, http://www.un.org/en/ga/search/view_doc.asp?symbol=A/RES/68/68.

"UNICORN Experiments Yield Crucial Data," *Nuclear Weapons Journal* (a publication of Los Alamos National Laboratory), Issue 2, 2006, pp. 20-21.

U.S. Air Force Research Laboratory and National Nuclear Security Administration. *Proceedings of the 30th Monitoring Research Review: Ground-Based Nuclear Explosion Monitoring Technologies,* September 23-25, 2008, Portsmouth, VA.

U.S. Congress. Congressional Research Service. CRS Report R41160, *North Korea's 2009 Nuclear Test: Containment, Monitoring, Implications*, by Jonathan E. Medalia.

U.S. Congress. Senate. *Comprehensive Nuclear Test-Ban Treaty: Message from the President of the United States Transmitting Comprehensive Nuclear Test-Ban Treaty ... ,* Treaty Doc. 105-28, September 23, 1997. Washington: GPO, 1997, xvi + 230 p.

U.S. Department of Defense. *Nuclear Posture Review Report.* April 2010, http://www.defense.gov/npr/docs/2010%20Nuclear%20Posture%20Review%20Report.pdf.

U.S. Department of Energy. *FY 2015 Congressional Budget Request.* volume 1, National Nuclear Security Administration, DOE/CF-0096, March 2014, http://www.energy.gov/sites/prod/files/2014/03/f12/Volume_1_NNSA.pdf.

U.S. Department of Energy. *United States Nuclear Tests: July 1945 through September 1992.* DOE/NV-209 (Rev. 15), December 2000: xviii + 162 p. http://www.nv.doe.gov/library/publications/historical/DOENV_209_REV15.pdf.

U.S. Department of Energy. *Fiscal Year 2015 Stockpile Stewardship and Management Plan,* Report to Congress, April 2014, http://nnsa.energy.gov/sites/default/files/nnsa/04-14-inlinefiles/2014-04-11%20FY15SSMP_FINAL_4-10-2014.pdf.

U.S. Department of Energy. National Nuclear Security Administration. "NNSA Conducts Pollux Subcritical Experiment at Nevada National Security Site," press release, December 6, 2012, http://www.nnsa.energy.gov/print/mediaroom/pressreleases/pollux120612.

U.S. Department of Energy. National Nuclear Security Administration. *Nuclear Test Readiness,* Report to Congress, May 2011, 6 p. + app.

U.S. Department of Energy. National Nuclear Security Administration, "Summary of Experiments Conducted in Support of Stockpile Stewardship," June 2014, (lists experiments by type for first two quarters of FY2014), 4 p., http://nnsa.energy.gov/sites/default/files/nnsa/06-14-inlinefiles/2014-06-04%20Quarterly%20SSP%20Experiment%20Summary-Q2FY14_complete_rjh%20final.pdf.

U.S. Secretary of Energy, Secretary of Defense, and Secretary of State. "National Security and Nuclear Weapons: Maintaining Deterrence in the 21st Century." July 2007, 3 p. http://www.nnsa.doe.gov/docs/factsheets/2007/NA-07-FS-04.pdf.

U.S. Department of State. "Remarks at the Friends of the Comprehensive Nuclear-Test-Ban Treaty Ministerial," John Kerry, Secretary of State, United Nations Headquarters, New York City, September 26, 2014, http://www.state.gov/secretary/remarks/2014/09/232219.htm.

U.S. White House. Office of the Press Secretary. "Joint Statement Between President George W. Bush and [Indian] Prime Minister Manmohan Singh," July 16, 2005.

Walter, Katie, "Sleuthing Seismic Signals," *Science & Technology Review,* March 2009, pp. 4-12.

Weapons of Mass Destruction Commission, *Weapons of Terror: Freeing the World of Nuclear, Biological and Chemical Arms.* June 2006, 227 p. http://www.wmdcommission.org/files/Weapons_of_Terror.pdf.

"The United States-Indonesia Comprehensive Partnership," speech by H.E. Dr. N. Hassan Wirajuda, Minister for Foreign Affairs, Republic of Indonesia, at a breakfast forum with the Carnegie Endowment for International Peace and USINDO, Washington, DC, June 8, 2009.

Woolsey, R. James, and Keith Payne, "Reconsidering the Comprehensive Test Ban Treaty: It's an Ineffectual Gesture That Could Do More Harm Than Good," *National Review Online,* September 8, 2011, http://www.nationalreview.com/articles/276530/reconsidering-comprehensive-test-ban-treaty-r-james-woolsey.

Appendix. Chronology, 1992-2009

09/23/92—The United States conducted its most recent nuclear test, "Divider."

10/02/92—President Bush signed the FY1993 Energy and Water Development Appropriations Act, P.L. 102-377; Section 507 restricted U.S. nuclear testing.

10/13/92—Russia announced an extension of its test moratorium at least to mid-1993.

01/13/93—President François Mitterrand said France would extend its test moratorium as long as the United States and Russia did.

04/24/93—At the Vancouver summit, Presidents Clinton and Yeltsin agreed that negotiations on a multilateral test ban should begin soon.

07/03/93—President Clinton announced his plan to continue the test moratorium through September 1994 as long as no other nation tests.

08/10/93—The Conference on Disarmament (CD) gave its Ad Hoc Committee on a Nuclear Test Ban a mandate to negotiate a CTBT.

10/05/93—China held the world's first nuclear test since September 1992.

01/25/94—The Conference on Disarmament opened its 1994 session in Geneva, with negotiation of a CTBT its top priority.

03/15/94—The United States extended its test moratorium through September 1995.

06/10/94—China conducted an underground nuclear test.

09/26/94—President Yeltsin, in an address to the U.N. General Assembly, said, "Russia favors signing this treaty [the CTBT] next year."

10/07/94—China conducted an underground nuclear test.

01/24/95—President Clinton said in his State of the Union address, "The United States will lead the charge to extend indefinitely the Nuclear Non-Proliferation Treaty [and] to enact a comprehensive nuclear test ban."

01/30/95—President Clinton continued the U.S. moratorium until a CTBT enters into force, assuming it is signed before September 30, 1996.

05/11/95—The Nuclear Non-Proliferation Treaty Review and Extension Conference agreed to extend that treaty indefinitely, and by reference called for completing CTBT negotiations not later than 1996.

05/15/95—China conducted a nuclear test, its fourth since September 1992.

06/13/95—President Jacques Chirac announced that France would conduct eight nuclear tests in the South Pacific between September 1995 and May 1996.

08/04/95—The Senate tabled, 56 to 44, an amendment by Senator Exon and others to delete $50 million for conducting hydronuclear tests (those producing extremely low nuclear yield). The amendment was to S. 1026, the FY1996 National Defense Authorization Bill.

08/10/95—France announced that once it completed its nuclear test program, it would support a CTBT that bans all nuclear tests of any yield.

08/11/95—President Clinton announced his decision to pursue a "true zero yield" CTBT, banning all nuclear tests regardless of yield, accompanied by six "safeguards" to assure confidence in U.S. nuclear weapons under a CTBT.

08/17/95—China conducted a nuclear test, its fifth since September 1992.

09/05/95—France conducted a nuclear test, its first since 1991.

12/13/95—A U.N. General Assembly resolution, passed 85-18, "strongly deplores" current nuclear testing and "strongly urges" an immediate end to testing.

01/23/96—In his State of the Union Address, President Clinton stated, "We must end the race to create new nuclear weapons by signing a truly comprehensive nuclear test ban treaty—this year."

01/27/96—France held the sixth nuclear test in its test series.

01/29/96—President Chirac announced "the final end to French nuclear tests."

03/07/96—The Washington *Times* reported U.S. intelligence agencies have ambiguous evidence that Russia may have conducted a nuclear test in January 1996.

04/19/96—President Yeltsin formally endorsed a zero-yield CTBT and reserved the right to resume testing if Russia's supreme interests are threatened. The next day, the Group of Seven plus Russia expressed their commitment to complete and sign a zero-yield CTBT by September 1996.

05/28/96—Ambassador Jaap Ramaker of the Netherlands, chairman of the CD's Ad Hoc Committee on a Nuclear Test Ban, tabled a draft text of a CTBT incorporating compromises on key outstanding issues.

06/04/96—France and the United States signed an agreement to share information relevant to maintaining nuclear weapons.

06/08/96—China held a nuclear test and declared that after one more test it would join an international moratorium on nuclear explosions.

06/20/96—India stated it would not sign a CTBT unless the five declared nuclear weapon states agreed to a timetable to give up their nuclear weapons.

06/26/96—The Senate tabled, 53-45, an amendment by Senators Kyl and Reid to the FY1997 National Defense Authorization Bill to permit U.S. nuclear testing after September 30, 1996, under certain conditions if the Senate had not given its advice and consent to ratification of a CTBT.

07/23/96—The United States and Russia announced their joint support for the existing draft CTBT. While this draft did not fully satisfy either nation, they saw it as acceptable and the only route to achieving a CTBT in 1996.

07/29/96—China conducted what it said would be its last nuclear test, and pledged to begin a moratorium on testing on July 30.

08/07/96—China and the United States reportedly reached an agreement on modifying the draft treaty so as to resolve China's concerns over CTBT verification, clearing the way for China to support the treaty.

08/20/96—India vetoed the draft CTBT in the CD, barring the treaty from going to the U.N. General Assembly as a CD document.

08/23/96—Australia asked the U.N. General Assembly to begin consideration of the draft CTBT on September 9.

09/10/96—The U.N. General Assembly adopted, 158 to 3 (with 5 abstentions and 19 nations not voting), the draft CTBT negotiated at the CD.

09/24/96—The CTBT was opened for signing; President Clinton and others signed.

11/20/96—The Preparatory Commission for the Comprehensive Test Ban Treaty Organization (CTBTO) began its first meeting.

07/02/97—The Department of Energy conducted its first subcritical experiment, "Rebound," at the Nevada Test Site. It conducted one more in 1997.

08/28/97—The *Washington Times* reported Administration officials as saying Russia may have conducted a nuclear explosion on August 16.

09/22/97—President Clinton submitted the CTBT to the Senate for its advice and consent to ratification.

11/04/97—The *Washington Post* reported the Administration formally dropped its claim that a seismic event of August 16, 1997, was a Russian nuclear test.

01/21/98—Senator Jesse Helms, in a letter to President Clinton, said "the CTBT is very low on the [Senate Foreign Relations] Committee's list of priorities."

01/27/98—In his State of the Union address, President Clinton asked the Senate to approve the CTBT this year and announced that four former Chairmen of the Joint Chiefs of Staff had endorsed the treaty.

03/25/98—The Department of Energy conducted its third subcritical experiment, "Stagecoach," at the Nevada Test Site. It conducted two more in 1998.

04/06/98—Britain and France became the first declared nuclear weapon states to ratify the CTBT, depositing instruments of ratification with the United Nations.

05/11/98—Prime Minister Vajpayee announced India conducted three nuclear tests.

05/13/98—India announced that it conducted two nuclear tests.

05/28/98—Pakistan announced that it conducted five nuclear tests.

05/30/98—Pakistan announced that it conducted one nuclear test.

06/05/98—The foreign ministers of China, France, Russia, the United Kingdom, and the United States, in a joint communique, condemned the Indian and Pakistani nuclear tests, urged India and Pakistan to refrain from weaponizing or deploying nuclear weapons, and called on them to adhere to the CTBT "immediately and unconditionally."

09/23/98—Pakistan's Prime Minister, Nawaz Sharif, in an address to the United Nations, said his nation would adhere to the CTBT if other nations lifted economic sanctions, as long as India refrained from testing.

12/00/98—Secretary of Energy Bill Richardson and Secretary of Defense William Cohen submitted the third annual nuclear stockpile certification memorandum to the President stating, "The nuclear stockpile has no safety or reliability concerns that require underground testing at this time."

02/09/99—The Department of Energy conducted its sixth subcritical experiment, "Clarinet," at the Nevada Test Site. It conducted two more in 1999.

05/25/99—The Cox Committee, in its report, stated its belief that China may be continuing to conduct underground nuclear tests.

07/20/99—In separate press conferences, President Clinton and nine Senators urged the Senate to consider the CTBT. A survey found 82% of Americans want the treaty approved. All 45 Democratic Senators wrote to Senator Helms urging him to hold hearings on the treaty and to report it to the Senate.

07/26/99—Responding to the July 20 letter, Senator Helms stated that "I do not share your enthusiasm for this treaty" and that the Senate Foreign Relations Committee would consider it after amendments to the ABM Treaty and the Kyoto Protocol.

09/30/99—Senator Lott proposed a unanimous-consent request that would bring the CTBT to the Senate floor for 10 hours of debate beginning October 6, and then to a vote.

10/08/99—(1) States that had ratified the CTBT ended a three-day conference on expediting entry into force. (2) The Senate began debate on the treaty.

10/11/99—President Clinton wrote to Senators Lott and Daschle to request that a vote on the CTBT be delayed.

10/13/99—The Senate rejected the CTBT, 48 for, 51 against, 1 present.

01/28/00—Secretary of State Albright announced that Gen. John Shalikashvili (ret.) would head the Administration's effort to achieve bipartisan support for CTBT ratification, but the State Department indicated the Administration did not expect to seek Senate approval of the treaty in 2000.

02/04/00—DOE conducted the ninth U.S. subcritical experiment, "Oboe 3." It held four more in 2000.

02/04/00—Russia announced that it conducted seven subcritical experiments between September 23, 1999, and January 8, 2000.

06/30/00—Russia ratified the CTBT.

11/03/00—Russia announced that it completed its fifth and final series of subcritical experiments for 2000 at Novaya Zemlya during the week of October 30.

01/17/01—Colin Powell, as nominee for Secretary of State, said the Administration would not ask for CTBT ratification in this session of Congress.

03/04/01—The *New York Times* reported U.S. intelligence experts were divided on whether Russia had conducted clandestine tests over the past several years.

06/26/01—The House Appropriations Committee declined to add funds to the FY2002 Energy and Water Development Appropriations Bill to increase nuclear test readiness, arguing the Secretary of Defense, President, Armed Services Committees, and Congress must first request or approve these funds.

09/26/01—The National Nuclear Security Agency (NNSA) held the 14th U.S. subcritical experiment, "Oboe 8." It conducted one more in 2001.

11/11/01—The Conference on Facilitating the Entry into Force of the CTBT began on this date at U.N. headquarters in New York and ended November 13.

02/15/02—NNSA held the 16th U.S. subcritical experiment, and the first with UK participation, "Vito." It conducted three more subcritical experiments, without UK participation, in 2002.

05/10/02—The House passed H.R. 4546, the Bob Stump National Defense Authorization Act for FY2003; it called for DOE to achieve the ability to conduct a nuclear test within a year of a presidential direction to test.

07/31/02—The National Academy of Sciences issued a report asserting that the main technical concerns raised in regard to the CTBT are manageable.

09/26/02—NNSA held the 19th U.S. subcritical experiment, "Rocco."

02/00/03—A House Policy Committee report recommended "a test readiness program that could achieve an underground diagnostic [nuclear] test within 18 months"; the Bipartisan Congressional Task Force on Nonproliferation urged President Bush "not to resume nuclear weapons testing."

05/22/03—The Senate passed, 98-1, S. 1050, the FY2004 National Defense Authorization Bill. Section 3132 directed the Secretary of Energy to achieve by October 1, 2006, and to maintain thereafter, the ability to conduct a nuclear test within 18 months of a decision to test, unless the Secretary determines that a different number of months is preferable.

09/00/03—A conference on facilitating the CTBT's entry into force was held in Vienna, Austria, September 3-5.

09/19/03—NNSA held the 20th U.S. subcritical experiment, "Piano."

10/30/03—The U.N. General Assembly's First Committee (Disarmament and International Security) approved a draft resolution, "A Path to Total Elimination of Nuclear Weapons," 146-2, with 16 abstentions. A provision stressed the importance of achieving early entry into force of the CTBT. The United States and India voted no; the U.S. representative stated that he did so because of U.S. opposition to the CTBT.

11/00/03—The 21st meeting of the CTBTO Preparatory Commission was held November 10-13 in Vienna, Austria.

12/08/03—The U.N. General Assembly adopted, 164-2, with 2 abstentions, a resolution, "A Path to Total Elimination of Nuclear Weapons."

01/06/04—Libya became the 109th nation to ratify the CTBT.

05/25/04—NNSA held the 21st U.S. subcritical experiment, "Armando."

06/20/04—In a joint statement, India and Pakistan agreed to reaffirm their unilateral moratoria on nuclear testing, barring extraordinary events, and to establish a dedicated and secure hotline between the two foreign secretaries.

06/00/04—The 22nd meeting of the CTBTO Preparatory Commission was held June 22-24 in Vienna, Austria.

09/24/04—Foreign ministers from 42 nations issue a statement calling entry into force of the CTBT "more urgent today than ever before."

12/03/04—The U.N. General Assembly adopted, 177-2, with 4 abstentions, a resolution, "Comprehensive Nuclear-Test-Ban Treaty."

02/10/05—North Korea declared, "We ... have manufactured nukes for self-defense to cope with the Bush Administration's evermore undisguised policy to isolate and stifle the DPRK."

03/10/05—The European Parliament passed a resolution that, among other things, "reiterates its call for the USA ... to sign and ratify the CTBT."

05/00/05—At the Nuclear Nonproliferation Treaty Review Conference, held May 2-27, some nations criticized the United States for not ratifying the CTBT.

05/16/05—The *New York Times* reported that on May 15, National Security Advisor Stephen Hadley stated, "Action would have to be taken" if North Korea conducted a nuclear test.

08/29/05—Egyptian Foreign Minister Ahmed Aboul Gheit reportedly stated that Egypt would not ratify the CTBT until Israel joins the NPT.

09/00/05—A conference, Facilitating the Entry into Force of the Comprehensive Nuclear Test Ban Treaty, was held September 21 to 23 at U.N. headquarters in New York.

11/00/05—The 25th session of the Preparatory Commission for the Comprehensive Nuclear-Test-Ban Treaty Organization was held November 14 to 18.

12/08/05—The U.N. General Assembly adopted, 168-2, a resolution on nuclear disarmament that, among other things, urged nations to ratify the CTBT.

2/23/06—The United States and United Kingdom conducted a subcritical experiment, "Krakatau," at the Nevada Test Site.

06/00/06—The 26th meeting of the Preparatory Commission for the Comprehensive Nuclear Test Ban Treaty Organization was held June 20-23.

08/30/06—The United States conducted its 23rd subcritical experiment, "Unicorn," at the Nevada Test Site.

09/20/06—Fifty-nine foreign ministers called on states that have not done so to ratify the treaty.

09/28/06—Representative Tauscher introduced H.Res. 1059, calling on the Senate to give its advice and consent to CTBT ratification.

10/03/06—North Korea declared that it will conduct a nuclear test.

10/09/06—North Korea claimed to have conducted its first nuclear test; most reports placed the explosive yield of the test at one kiloton or less.

10/16/06—The United States confirmed that the North Korean event of October 9 was a nuclear test.

11/17/06—The Preparatory Commission for the Comprehensive Nuclear-Test-Ban Treaty Organization concluded its 27th meeting.

01/04/07—Four former government officials urged "[i]nitiating a bipartisan process with the Senate ... to achieve ratification of the Comprehensive Test Ban Treaty."

01/31/07—Mikhail Gorbachev called on nuclear weapon states to ratify the CTBT.

03/29/07—The Comprehensive Nuclear-Test-Ban Treaty Organization Preparatory Commission certified the 200th and 201st International Monitoring System stations.

06/04/07—The Senate Armed Services Committee reported S. 1547, FY2008 National Defense Authorization Act. Section 3122, Sense of Congress on the Nuclear Nonproliferation Policy of the United States and the Reliable Replacement Warhead Program, included a provision, "the Senate should ratify the Comprehensive Nuclear-Test-Ban Treaty."

06/04/07—The United States paid $10.0 million toward the International Monitoring System to the Comprehensive Test Ban Treaty Organization Preparatory Commission.

06/22/07—The Preparatory Commission for the Comprehensive Nuclear-Test-Ban Treaty Organization concluded its 28th meeting.

09/00/07—The United Nations held the fifth conference on facilitating CTBT entry into force on September 17 and 18 in Vienna, Austria.

10/24/07—Senator Jon Kyl delivered a speech critical of the CTBT and of Section 3122 of H.R. 1585, the FY2008 National Defense Authorization Act, expressing the sense of Congress that the Senate should ratify the CTBT. Senator Kyl included a letter signed by 41 Senators opposing the treaty and Section 3122.

11/14/07—The Preparatory Commission for the Comprehensive Nuclear-Test-Ban Treaty Organization concluded its 29th meeting.

11/19/07—Former Secretary of Defense Harold Brown and former Director of Central Intelligence John Deutch suggested a five-year renewable CTBT in lieu of the current treaty.

12/05/07—By a vote of 176 for, 1 against (United States), and 4 abstentions, the U.N. General Assembly adopted resolution A/RES/62/59 stressing the importance of achieving the earliest entry into force of the CTBT.

11/26/07—The conference report on H.R. 1585, the FY2008 defense authorization bill, was ordered to be printed. The bill provided for biennial reports on U.S. nuclear test readiness and dropped a provision in the Senate bill expressing the sense of Congress that "the Senate should ratify" the CTBT.

12/17/07—Representative Tauscher introduced H.Res. 882, expressing the sense of the House that the Senate should initiate a bipartisan process to give its advice and consent to ratification of the CTBT.

01/29/08—Colombia, one of the Annex 2 states that must ratify the CTBT for it to enter into force, became the 144th nation to ratify the treaty.

02/25/08—The United States paid $23.8 million to the Comprehensive Nuclear-Test-Ban Treaty Preparatory Commission, restoring its voting rights in the commission.

05/27/08—Senator John McCain said he would "tak[e] another look at the Comprehensive Test Ban Treaty to see what can be done to overcome the shortcomings that prevented it from entering into force."

06/26/08—The Preparatory Commission for the Comprehensive Nuclear-Test-Ban Treaty Organization concluded its 30th meeting.

08/19/08—Iraq became the 179th nation to sign the CTBT.

09/00/08—The Preparatory Commission for the Comprehensive Nuclear-Test-Ban Treaty Organization conducted a large-scale Integrated Field Exercise in Kazakhstan to simulate a complete on-site inspection.

09/24/08—A joint ministerial statement urging states that have not done so to sign and ratify the CTBT was launched; as of December 12, 2008, 96 nations had associated themselves with the statement.

11/21/08—Lebanon became the 148th nation to ratify the CTBT.

01/13/09—In her answers to questions for the record prepared for her confirmation hearing of this date, Secretary of State-designate Hillary Clinton said, "The President-Elect and I are both strongly committed to Senate approval of the CTBT and to launching a diplomatic effort to bring on board other states whose ratifications are required for the treaty to enter into force."

04/05/09—In a speech in Prague, President Obama said, "my administration will immediately and aggressively pursue U.S. ratification of the Comprehensive Test Ban Treaty."

05/25/09—North Korea announced that it had conducted a nuclear test, its second.

06/08/09—Foreign Minister Hassan Wirajuda of Indonesia said that his nation would "immediately" ratify the CTBT once the United States did so.

06/10/09—An international scientific conference was held in Vienna, Austria, June 10-12 to present the results of the International Scientific Studies project.

09/00/09—A conference on CTBT entry into force, pursuant to Article XIV of the treaty, was held at U.N. headquarters in New York on September 24 and 25.

Author Contact Information

Jonathan E. Medalia
Specialist in Nuclear Weapons Policy
jmedalia@crs.loc.gov, 7-7632